Stitch 'n Swap

25 Handmade Projects to Sew, Give & Receive

Generation Q Magazine
Compiled by Jake Finch

stashBOOKS.

an imprint of C&T Publishing

Text copyright © 2014 by Jake Finch

Photography and Artwork copyright © 2014 by C&T Publishing, Inc.

Publisher: Amy Marson

Creative Director: Gailen Runge

Art Director/Cover Designer: Kristy Zacharias

Book Designer: Casey Dukes

Editor: S. Michele Fry

Technical Editors: Helen Frost and Amanda Siegfried

Production Coordinator: Rue Flaherty

Production Editor: Joanna Burgarino

Illustrator: Wendy Mathson

Photo Assistant: Mary Peyton Peppo

Styled photos by Nissa Brehmer, unless otherwise noted; Instructional photos by Diane Pedersen, unless otherwise noted

Published by Stash Books, an imprint of C&T Publishing, Inc., P.O. Box 1456, Lafayette, CA 94549

Library of Congress Cataloging-in-Publication Data

Stitch 'n swap : 25 handmade projects to sew, give & receive / Generation Q magazine ; compiled by Jake Finch, leader of the GenQ Team.

  pages cm

ISBN 978-1-60705-849-6 (soft cover)

1. Sewing. 2. Gifts. 3. Games. I. Finch, Jake, 1967- editor of compilation. II. Title: Stitch and swap.

TT715.S75 2014

646.2--dc23

                          2013040403

Printed in China

10 9 8 7 6 5 4 3 2 1

Contents

ACKNOWLEDGMENTS

Generation Q Magazine is first and foremost a community. Community helped us launch into print, and community is again the backbone of this book. From our staff and contributing designers to our tolerant alter egos at C&T Publishing—who stood eagerly ready to receive this manuscript's many pieces—we can't thank our peeps enough. We can't tell you how often our staff rushed bravely into the deadline battlefield to help us with one more idea or one last missing piece so that those at C&T—publisher (Amy), editors (Roxane, Michele, and Gailen), designers, and photographers could wave their respective magic cursors and make a book. And we hope you know that our gratitude is wrapped in awe and humility of everyone's incredible talent.

At the end of the day, though, it will be our Q-bies—our sisters and brothers of the cloth—whom we really thank the most. Without your support, we would not be here to write this book and hand it over to you all, hoping that it serves your needs.

ABOUT *GENERATION Q MAGAZINE*

Founded in 2010 by Jake Finch and Melissa Thompson Maher, *Generation Q Magazine* is a community of modern and contemporary quilters, sewists, and crafters who revel in their creativity and want to share the fun with anyone who will bother to play with them.

As a magazine, e-zine, website, and pattern publisher (print and digital), *GenQ* seeks to inspire, delight, challenge, instruct, reflect, and report on what makes us creative stitchers tick. In a style sometimes cheeky, other times insightful, our mission is to entertain and inform the masses, to hopefully convert the most stalwart sewing critics into fiber minions, and to ultimately take over the world with quilts. We are *GenQ*.

Check us out at GenerationQMagazine.com, and find us in your local quilt shop, bookstore, or newsstand. Then you can join us for all of the fun!

Jake Finch—Compiler

Jake's fabric addiction started when she traded her credit cards for a sewing machine back in the early years of her marriage to Stephen. A quarter century later, she now has several machines, and several credit cards, but they are only used for stash improvement. A journalist by training and a self-taught quilter and sewist, Jake can't believe that she's been able to blend all of her interests into a deeply satisfying career (as the publisher of *GenQ*) that allows her to be home with Samantha, work with her closest friends, and receive more fabric, books, and thread than she can use. Which is why *GenQ's* readers routinely get them.

Website: MamaMakesQuilts.com

INTRODUCTION

swap

noun

    an act, instance, or process of exchanging one thing for another

verb

    to give in trade; to exchange

One of the best aspects of belonging to a community of like-minded stitchers (think guild, bee, small group, or other regular congregation of those you have something in common with), whether online or in real time, is having the opportunity to share your talents and creativity. Swaps provide a fun, give-and-take format that allows for the sharing of talent in a tangible way. A side benefit that has made them so popular is the friendships and bonds that develop among participants, even across fiber-optic lines.

Swaps are organized around a theme and a set of rules. In a swap, each participant is both a giver and a receiver of the swap's project. Usually, the participants only know to whom they are giving their finished project, but there are no hard rules for this. It's at the reveal, when the projects are exchanged, that the mystery is solved.

What sets this apart from a challenge is the exchange part. With challenges you generally keep what you make; swapping provides a challenge, plus the joy of gift making, giving, and receiving. The core purpose of participating in a swap event is to have fun. It's a sewing game!

And that's why so many varied themes and ways to play are part of the swap process. The theme of a swap can be just about anything that you can imagine—a single fabric, a fabric collection, a color, a holiday, a room, and so on. A swap can be around a technique (maybe raw-edge appliqué) or an item (such as pincushions or doll quilts). The item might need to have a purpose (storage) or be specific to a room (kitchen). You can even combine themes—whatever floats your group's boat. There is no end to why, how, and what is traded among players.

Every other reason—creative exploration, camaraderie, showcasing talent or new techniques—is irrelevant if you and your group lose sight of the fun factor. That's right. It's all about the fun, people.

One major thing to know about swaps is that usually the projects are small and easy. In our opinion, if you can't complete your swap project in less than a day (except if you're a newbie stitcher or trying a new technique), then the swap is going to inflict stress instead of bringing joy, and that's not good. Small projects mean small pieces of fabrics; precuts or scraps are great.

Here at *Generation Q Magazine* (*GenQ* to our friends, and that's *you*!) we're addicted to swaps and individually join the ones that strike our fancy. We get a kick out of hosting swaps among our readers, too. And we've lurked around the many Flickr pages and blog posts that show off other groups' wonderful swaps. We're repeatedly amazed at the creativity and joy that come from swap participation.

So where do you start? Well, Q-bie, that's what we're here for. We'll give you ideas and inspiration to start your own swap effort among your creative groups, and we'll happily cheer you on as you work through the process. And because this book is all about the sharing of ideas, we've brought in some of our favorite talented stitching people to give us some jumping-off points for your creativity. Some fabulous projects fill the following pages, and all of them can be adapted to *your* taste, *your* style, and *your* skill and creativity level. Don't limit yourself; make it your own unique project. C'mon, we dare you!

Jake, Melissa, and the *GenQ* Team

Organizing a Swap

So you think you want to launch a swap, eh? Cool! We're right there with you on this. We promise that at the end of this effort, you'll be dazzled and amazed by how creative and talented your Q-buds are, and even more likely, you'll know the feeling of rising up to and meeting a challenge.

Any type of sewing/quilting challenge should stretch your creative muscles. After all, you're given a prescribed set of rules to follow, and in all likelihood, you wouldn't have rules—not these rules at least—determining how to spend your sewing time.

Here's a list of what you need to get your swap started:

- A group of like-minded stitchers who want to play with you, and someone willing to be in charge.

- A start date and deadline for the swap's completion.

- Clear details about the swap's theme/project.

- Written guidelines for your participants to refer back to as they work on their projects. This will include the swap theme or premise, the pertinent dates, the contact person for questions, requirements for the finished project, and information about the reveal.

- A list indicating who will swap with whom.

- A backup plan in case anyone has to drop out (page 11).

The following suggestions are optional, but we think they're helpful for swap success:

- Develop an email system or some type of contact list that includes each participant so you can update them on any changes or remind them of deadlines.

- Create a community page online (on a site like Flickr, Facebook, or Pinterest), where images of your swap results can be shared.

- In a face-to-face swap, appoint someone to take pictures of the finished projects and the receivers.

- If you're working with a particular fabric or product, you might want to partner with an online or brick-and-mortar shop where more of the material can be purchased. Also, you can contact the manufacturers to see if they will provide you the materials for free or at a reduced cost. Many manufacturers understand the promotional value of a swap.

- If you're using a specific pattern, assuming that it is copyright-free, provide the web address so your participants can find it. In person, you could provide a printout of the pattern.

- If you're using someone's commercial or published pattern, contact that designer or publication and ask for written permission to use the pattern. This isn't just common courtesy; this is a potential legal issue. Most designers and publishers will be happy to give you their nod, especially if you're giving them credit.

Who's Playing with You?

The core of a swap is the people who participate. It's all about community, folks, whether you lay eyes on these people every week or month, or you just talk to them online. Community is what makes a swap different from a challenge. You're sharing your talents with another person.

With this in mind, a swap can be organized with as few as three people or as many as you have the brain cells to coordinate. We think a comfortable number for a first-time endeavor is about twenty people. That's enough bodies to have some really fun things made for the swap, and enough people that you can turn to another participant if someone drops out. (More on this later.) Also, twenty people are not too difficult to keep track of. But remember: You're not their mommy or daddy; you're just the facilitator.

It's not just big girls and boys who like swapping! If you happen to have any kids in your group, are a 4-H or Scout leader, or have a young guild with little ones around, the youth could do their own swap. Or you could do an adult-child swap. Projects in this book that would be particularly apt for that: pot holders, eye pillows, pincushions, the monster (of course), and the doll quilts and pillow.

Pick out a method for getting better acquainted with partners in the swap. Often a set of questions is circulated. This is part of the fun, too. Have everyone answer get-to-know-you questions, specifically about things that might apply to your swap. Do you like lace or denim? What are your favorite and hated colors? What size and type of bag do you prefer? What hot drink do you like best? Are you allergic to anything? Additional questions might just be fun but could give you some insight—and ideas for their swap gift and any other treats you might include. Just think of the things you would learn if they tell you their dream vacation spot, favorite weekend activity, or favorite Pinterest board.

How you conduct the question-and-answer part of your swap can be almost as varied as the type of swap. Paper or online? Through your facilitator or by having the same questions answered by everyone in an open, online forum?

What Are You Playing?

Once you have an interested group of playmates, decide what your swap will be. And guess what: that's what this whole book is about—ideas for swaps. But don't be limited by what we've provided. We'll consider this book a success if our ideas inspire you in some way to create your own unique swap.

THEMES

We've said it before, but hey, repetition is our friend: a swap can be organized around a ton of different themes. Here are just some of the more popular ideas:

- Common fabric: A designer, a type of print, someone's "uglies"
- How the project will be used
- Holiday or special occasion
- The recipient (new parent, child, student)
- A supporting product (special interfacing, buttons, found objects)
- Size
- Color
- Quilt block
- Type of project (wallets, pincushions, pillows)
- A quote or poem

You can even take two or more of these and group them together in a swap. For example, we know of a guild that used paint chips to organize a challenge. Each participant drew two chips and was allowed to add one more color to the mix. Then they created a small quilt from the colors. You could easily adapt this idea to a swap.

Another guild we're involved with had each participant give a fat quarter of fabric and a note saying what kind of small sewn item they wanted (pillow, bag, place mats). The person drawing the name/fabric then used their "swapee's" fabric in that finished product. The "what" of the project was open to the recipient's desire, and the desired item and provided fabric directed the person making it. (A few people in this swap said they didn't care what they received as long as the fabric was used.)

Pillows are a great swap theme because they are small, offer a blank slate, and are used by many people. Heather Bostic's *Pillow Pop*, published by Stash Books, is a great place to find pillow patterns.

STYLES

- Swaps can be organized like Secret Santa, where the participants are randomly given someone in the group to sew for.

- In a Leapfrog Swap, usually the person who will receive the swap project is not the same person who will make a project for the giver. This is more like a chain: Swapper A gives to Swapper B. Swapper B gives to Swapper C. And so on.

- People could be partnered, so they make something for each other.

- A Yankee-Style Swap is also a great way to make the exchanges. Unlike a traditional Secret Santa–type game, you don't know who you are making your gift for; it could go to anyone. You pick gifts one at a time and blindly—at least in person—and then the next person chooses an unknown gift or "steals" a known gift. One of the things that makes this work so well is that people try to create the most wonderful, most-likely-to-be-stolen gift.

- Of course, there are more; use your imagination or research skills!

Except for Yankee-Style, it's up to the group to determine if participants know who is sewing for them. Often identities are kept secret until the reveal.

Speaking of the reveal, we think this is the second-best part (next to getting the handmade items, natch). This is when everyone learns who they have been playing with. It can be a lot of fun to have secrets in a swap until the end, much like having a secret admirer. But at least one person—usually the organizer—always needs to know who is partnered with whom. That way, if someone drops out or can't participate in the reveal, then the organizer can step in and direct things appropriately so no one feels slighted.

ADVICE FOR A SUCCESSFUL SWAP

Type A Personality: Emily Herrick of Crazy Old Ladies said that, for her, the most important thing for a successful swap was having somebody very organized and committed at the lead, especially if there are a lot of people involved or if you're doing an online swap.

Keep It Simple: Offer a project that can be made relatively quickly, assuming your players all have intermediate sewing/quilting skills. If the swap project will take weeks or months to complete, you'll probably have a very limited pool of participants.

Supplies: All of these projects were developed with the assumption that the reader has basic sewing/quilting knowledge as well as basic tools—pins and needles, rotary cutter and mat, scissors for fabric and paper, measuring and marking tools—at hand. Anything not basic we've listed in the project's materials and supplies list.

If you are working around a set product, fabric, or tool that has been supplied by the swap, make sure there are extras for emergencies or surprises. For example, if your swap revolves around a specific charm pack of fabric and the swap organizer is disbursing those to participants, have at least a few extra packs. People lose things. Cars get stolen. Food gets spilled in sewing rooms. You just never know.

It is perfectly acceptable to ask participants to contribute to the cost of any bulk materials you're acquiring for the swap (such as charm square packs), but you need to respect your participants' wallets and outline the potential cost beforehand. If your group is resistant, plenty of swap ideas work around found objects or having each participant throw something into the mix (fat quarters, ribbons, their own scraps). The most important thing here is the communication. Clarity will cure potential problems.

Reminders: Offering regular email reminders to your participants will help keep everyone on track. Offering a tip or progress report or some tidbit with each reminder might keep people who are on track from getting annoyed with you for the reminders.

Drop-Off Plan: Along these same lines, if you are doing your reveal in person, make sure to set up a drop spot for anyone who can't be at the reveal event so they can leave their swap project for the recipient.

Dealing with Dropouts

Be prepared for having people drop out of the swap or flake altogether, and don't let it ruin your fun. This is where the swap organizer can make all of the difference in the remaining participants' experience. We suggest that the organizer stay out of the initial partnering up and instead make at least one if not two extra swap items following the swap guidelines. If you have a very big swap and people drop out early on, you can pair up the "leftover" participants. But you still need to have a backup swap project. Gracefully accepting when someone drops out will keep attitudes in check as well. Sometimes life just gets in the way of good intentions, and it's better to believe that a person dropping out is facing big hurdles; no need to write them off and chat about their dereliction to the other swap participants. That's why having a backup plan and project is so important.

Kaleidoscope PINCUSHION

Pincushions might well be the most perfect swap project. They are small, highly personal, and completely useful. They can be fashioned from endless shapes and materials and are perfect for both the beginner and established sewist. They also offer multiple ways to work a swap. Personally, we can't have enough pincushions and have five or six at the ready. Use each for a different type of pin or needle—machine, straight, hand. Also, they make adorable collectibles.

Made by Jeni Baker

Finished size: 5″ × 5″

Artist: Jeni Baker
Website: incolororder.com

Swap IDEAS

- For Kaleidoscope, a traditional Nine-Patch block was altered to become something fresh and different. It would be perfect for an Altered Block Swap.

- Another pincushion example, Wordplay, inspires other swap ideas. With a group whose members know one another pretty well, each sewist could  fashion a pincushion featuring one word that positively describes the recipient. The swap gift then becomes a positive affirmation for the recipient every time he or she sees it.

- Pincushions are great for a swap that involves just a few people, for instance, your bee, retreat, or mini-group. Because pincushions are so simple, put them together production-line style, and make one for each person in your group.

Jeni loves to find ways to be creative every day, whether through photography, sewing, or quilting. She started sewing when she was eleven years old. Recently she entered the world of fabric design as a licensed designer for Art Gallery Fabrics. She also writes and publishes sewing and quilting patterns under her own name. In her spare time, Jeni enjoys collecting vintage kitchenware and spending time with her pet bunny, George.

INSTRUCTIONS

All seam allowances are ¼".

1. Arrange and sew the squares into 2 Nine-Patch blocks. Press the seams open.

2. Sew the Nine-Patch blocks, right sides together, on all 4 sides.

3. Cut the blocks diagonally twice.

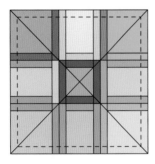

4. Open the pieces and press the seams open.

5. Arrange and sew 2 rows of 2 pieced squares each. Join the rows. Press the seams open.

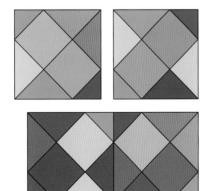

MATERIALS AND SUPPLIES

Solid fabric scraps: 18 squares 2" × 2"

Backing fabric: 6" × 6"

Filling (polyfill or crushed walnut shells)

6. Layer the pieced pincushion top with the 6" × 6" backing, right sides together. Trim any excess backing. Sew around all 4 sides, leaving a 1" opening along a side.

7. Turn right side out, clipping the corners and poking them out with a dull pencil. Stuff the pincushion as desired, and hand stitch the opening closed.

Sewing KIT

We could start a whole other addiction! Sewing kits are dreamy, offering us the sweetest places to keep our treasured tools. And they are practical because most of us move with our sewing at some point, even if it's just from the sewing machine to the family room to remind our tribe that we still exist. Michelle's goodies stitch up in an afternoon. For a lifetime-friendship guarantee, fill up your goodie bag with extra treats, like a few of your favorite brand of needles, some fabric scraps, and chocolate, of course!

Finished sizes:

Goodie Bag: 6˝ wide × 8˝ high × 4˝ deep

Rotary Case: 3˝ × 7½˝

Needle Book (closed): 4½˝ × 5˝

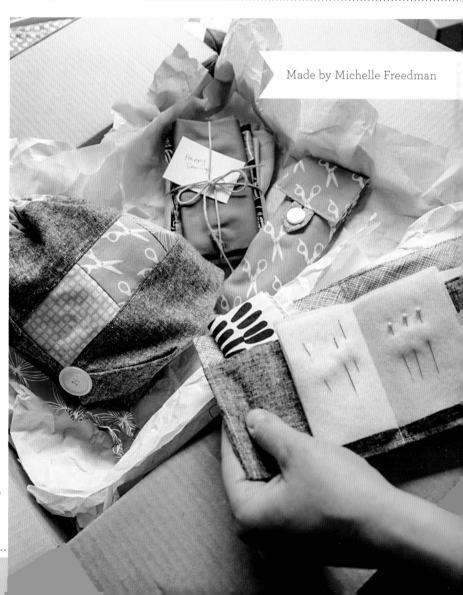

Made by Michelle Freedman

Artist: Michelle Freedman

Blog: designcamppdx.blogspot.com

Swap IDEA

Let's do a Round Robin Swap. To do this, create teams of four swapees, and set aside a couple of months. Give brown shopping bags to each person at the swap's start. At the kickoff meeting, each person puts several of his or her favorite sewing tools into the bag. Or you can designate which tools go in, such as a rotary cutter or seam ripper. (Please be careful with sharp stuff, people.) The bags are labeled with the starting person's name and handed off to the next person on the team. That person has one month (or whatever period of time you set) to make one thing to hold any or all of the items in the bag. At the next meeting, the bag is passed on to the next person, and this continues until all three team members have filled the bag with a handmade item for the starting person. Since everyone participates, each person will end up with three swap items made for their sewing basket. Oh, and the starting person is not allowed to see the progress in the bag until the end, but the three teammates can absolutely coordinate efforts if they don't want to work solo.

Michelle is an Oregon-based designer and author with a passion for making quilts. Her work has been featured in a variety of sewing and quilting publications. Michelle is the 2013 president of the Portland Modern Quilt Guild and the advertising manager for *Generation Q Magazine*.

MATERIALS AND SUPPLIES

Dark gray: ⅓ yard of cotton/linen for the bag, pocket, and needle book

Red print: ½ yard for the bag patchwork, lining, and ties

Gray print: fat quarter for the bag patchwork, casings, and rotary case

Yellow print: fat quarter for the bag patchwork, pocket, and rotary case lining

Light red print: fat quarter for the bag patchwork, needle book lining, and tabs

Felt sheet: 9″ × 12″ for the needle book

2 large buttons for the bag

2 medium shank buttons for the rotary case and needle book

Embroidery thread and needle

CUTTING

Dark gray

- Cut 1 rectangle 3½″ × 10½″ for the bag top.
- Cut 1 rectangle 10½″ × 15″ for the bag bottom.
- Cut 1 rectangle 5″ × 7″ for the bag inside pocket.
- Cut 1 rectangle 9½″ × 10″ for the needle book.

Red print

- Cut 1 square 2½″ × 2½″ for the bag patchwork.
- Cut 1 rectangle 10½″ × 20″ for the bag lining.
- Cut 2 strips 2″ × 30″ for the bag ties.

Gray print

- Cut 1 rectangle 2½″ × 3″ for the bag patchwork.
- Cut 2 rectangles 3″ × 10″ for the bag casings.
- Cut 1 rectangle 3½″ × 18″ for the rotary cutter case.

Yellow print

- Cut 1 rectangle 2½″ × 3½″ for the bag patchwork.
- Cut 1 rectangle 5″ × 4″ for the bag inside pocket.
- Cut 1 rectangle 3½″ × 18″ for the rotary cutter case lining.

Light red print

- Cut 1 rectangle 2½″ × 3″ for the bag patchwork.
- Cut 1 rectangle 2″ × 8″ for the needle book and rotary cutter case tabs.
- Cut 1 rectangle 9½″ × 10″ for the needle book lining.

Felt fabric

- Cut 2 rectangles 3½″ × 5″ for the needle book.

TIP

Because you're cutting for all three projects, prep separate bags to hold the pieces, one for each project.

Goodie Bag
INSTRUCTIONS

All seam allowances are ¼″ unless otherwise noted.

1. Sew together the 2½″ edges of the bag patchwork pieces, right sides together, to create a row. Press all the seams to the same side.

2. Sew the bag top and bottom pieces on either side of the pieced row. Press toward the bag fabric, and topstitch next to the seams on the dark gray fabric.

3. Fold the seamed outer fabric piece in half crosswise with right sides together. Match the raw edges and pin. Sew each side, leaving the top open.

4. To make the pocket, sew the dark gray 5″ × 7″ pocket piece to the yellow 5″ × 4″ pocket piece, right sides together, along a 5″ edge. Press the seams toward the gray. Topstitch. Fold the pocket in half, right sides together. Stitch along 2 sides, leaving the bottom open. Turn the pocket right side out and press.

5. With the pocket facing down, place the raw edges on the 10½″ × 20″ lining piece, 6½″ down from the top edge and about 3″ in from each side. Sew across the pocket bottom, securing it to the lining. Flip the pocket up toward the lining top and press. Topstitch the pocket to the lining on each side, securing it with a backstitch at the top and bottom edges.

6. To make the casings, fold the short ends of the 3″ × 10″ gray print pieces ½″ under to the fabric's wrong side. Press. Topstitch ⅜″ from the folds.

7. Fold the casings in half lengthwise, right sides out, and press. Center the casings on the short ends of the lining piece, right sides together, matching the raw edges, and baste in place. The casings will be shorter than the lining.

8. Fold the lining in half crosswise, right sides together, matching the raw edges, and pin. Mark a 2″ opening on a side. Sew both sides, leaving the 2″ opening. Press.

9. Place the lining fabric inside the outer bag, right sides together, matching the upper raw edges. Line up the side seams, and pin them in place. Continue to pin around the upper edges. Sew them together using a ½″ seam allowance.

10. Pull the outer bag right side out through the opening in the lining. Sew the opening closed. Gently poke out the corners of the bag using a dull pencil.

11. Press the top edge of the bag, and topstitch on the gray fabric to secure the casings.

12. Create box corners on the bag by folding the bag at a corner, matching up the side seam and bottom fold to create a triangle. Bring the triangle point up to the bottom edge of the pieced row and press. Sew a large button on the corner point. Repeat on the opposite side.

13. To make the bag's ties, fold the 2″ × 30″ red print pieces in half along the length, right sides together, and press. Sew the long edges. With a safety pin, turn the pieces right side out, press, and knot each end.

14. Attach a safety pin to an end of a tie, and thread it through both casings, exiting next to where it started. Repeat with the second tie in the opposite direction. Even up the tie ends, and knot them together.

—Fold.

Rotary Case
INSTRUCTIONS

All seam allowances are ¼″ unless otherwise noted.

1. To make the button tabs, fold the 2″ × 8″ light red print strip in half lengthwise, right sides together. Sew the long edges. Turn to the right side with a safety pin and press.

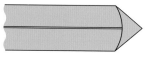

2. Cut the piece into 2 pieces 4″ long. Fold each piece to create a triangle at the top with 2 tails, and press. (Set a tab aside to use for the needle book).

3. Place the 3½″ × 18″ dark gray and yellow pieces right sides together, matching the raw edges. Sew along a short side. Press the seam toward the yellow, and topstitch through both fabrics.

4. Measure and mark 15″ from the seam on the yellow. Bring the seam to the mark. Fold the dark gray piece right side down over the other layers, and line up the short ends. Pin and sew just the long sides, leaving the top edges and folded ends open.

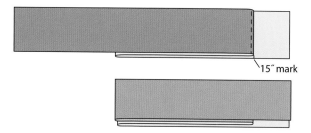

15″ mark

5. Turn right side out through the top edge opening. Gently push out the corners.

6. Press the ends of the top opening ½″ to the inside. Center the tab's ends between the layers ½″ to the inside. Pin in place, and topstitch the edge closed.

7. Mark the location of the shank button, and sew it to the rotary case. Be sure to catch only the top layers.

Needle Book
INSTRUCTIONS

All seam allowances are ¼˝ unless otherwise noted.

1. Place the 9½˝ × 10˝ gray and light red print pieces right sides together, matching the raw edges. Sew along a 10˝ edge. Press the seam toward the gray, and topstitch through both fabrics.

2. Place the button tab on the right side of the gray fabric, 2˝ down from the top edge. Match the raw edges (the point should be facing in) and baste.

3. Measure and mark 7½˝ from the seam on the red print. Bring the seam to the mark. Fold the gray piece right side down over the other layers, and line up the ends. Pin and sew the sides and top edge, leaving a 1½˝ opening on the side opposite the tab. Leave the folded ends open.

4. Clip the top corners and turn right side out through the opening. Gently push out the corners. Press and topstitch around all 4 sides.

5. Mark the needle book's center. Mark the center of a felt piece. Lay both felt pieces over the center of the needle book, and pin. Sew through all layers to create the felt pages, backstitching along the top and bottom edges.

6. With a long running stitch, embroider the outside of the needle book, catching just the dark gray fabric.

7. Mark the location for the shank button, and sew it to the needle book, catching just the dark gray fabric.

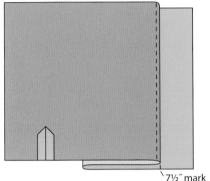

7½˝ mark

Woolly PIN SAVER AND SCISSOR CASE

Don't know about you, but we're always looking for our small scissors and snips. This adorable, simple scissor case is just the thing to keep us sane. And the great woolly pin saver is one of Rose's specialties. She turns these little, warm gems into jewelry, embellishments, and other things, but we like it here best as a mini-pincushion attached to the ribbon.

Made by Rose Hughes

Finished sizes:

Pin Saver: 2˝ × 2˝

Case: 2½˝ × 6½˝

Artist: Rose Hughes
Website: rosehughes.com
Blog: RavenSpeakQuilts.blogspot.com

Swap IDEA

If you have a passion for fabric and thread, you likely also harbor a not-so-secret love of small scissors. It's a shared love, believe us. So how about hosting a swap where each person has to hunt out a great pair of small scissors for his or her recipient and then fashion one of these cases to go with it? It's a perfect idea for the holidays, and many unique and fun scissors can be found on the Net.

Rose, of RavenSpeak Quilts, brings life's landscapes alive through her seemingly magically stitched together art quilts. She uses her simple method, called Fast Piece Appliqué, and has shared this and other fabri-magic in her teaching, patterns, and books. She lives in Paducah, Kentucky, with her husband, David, and two wonderful studio cats.

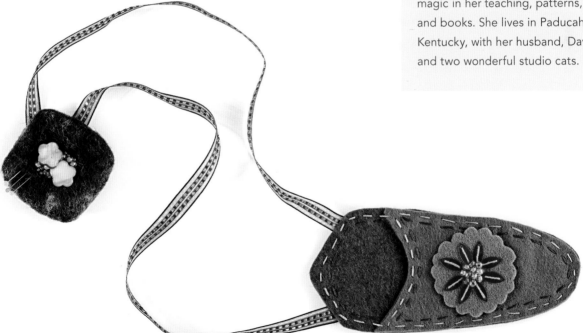

MATERIALS AND SUPPLIES

2 ropes of wool roving about 2″
(Rose used 2 purples—light and dark.)

4 or 5 squares 2″ × 2″ of cotton batting

Small scraps of felt

1 knee-high nylon stocking

Washing machine for the felting process

Laundry soap

Beads for embellishing

The Pin Saver

INSTRUCTIONS

1. Pull small wisps of the main color of wool roving, and spread it delicately out into a relatively flat layer.

2. Repeat this 5 or 6 times, placing each subsequent layer of roving perpendicular to the one prior to it and adding layers of highlight color as desired. (This directional layering will help bind all the fibers together during the felting process).

3. Stack the batting pieces on the center of the layered roving, gently wrapping the batting with the fibers.

4. Repeat Step 2, wrapping the batting from the opposite side.

5. Gently tuck the wool in around the wrapped batting, and place it into the stocking, tying a knot to hold it in place.

Felting the Bundle

To felt wool, moisture, heat, and pressure are combined to turn raw wool fibers (roving, in this case) into a matted wool fabric.

1. Place the stocking-wrapped bundle in a washing machine along with soapy hot water, and set it for high agitation. (Throwing the stocking in with a load of towels works great.)

2. Once the washer has stopped, remove the wool from its knotted stocking and air dry it. Then trim any loose fibers.

FINISHING

1. With beads and buttons, embellish the front of the pin saver as desired. Pass the threads through to the back side of the pin saver.

2. Cut a small piece of felt a little smaller than the pin saver. (It's hard to give a specific size, as each pin saver will be unique after the felting process.) Then cut a second piece of felt a little narrower than the first.

3. Tack stitch the corners of the larger felt piece to the back of the pin saver. Then stitch the narrower felt piece onto the larger piece, matching top and bottom edges. This will create a small sleeve.

MATERIALS AND SUPPLIES

Light green felt: 9″ × 12″ piece

Dark green felt: 9″ × 12″ piece

Purple felt: 2½″ × 2½″ square

⅜″ fun ribbon: ¾ yard

Embroidery thread

Beads

CUTTING

The patterns are on page 26. Trace and cut each pattern piece from tracing paper or template plastic.

Light green felt

■ Cut 2 front panels.

Dark green felt

■ Cut 2 back panels.

Purple felt

■ Cut 1 flower.

The Case
INSTRUCTIONS

1. Pin the purple flower in place on a light green front panel.

2. Stitch the beads in place through both layers. Add additional embellishments as desired.

3. Place the embellished front panel on top of the other light green front panel, and pin it in place.

4. Use a running stitch along the top curved edge of the pinned panels. (Rose did 2 rows of running stitches in different colors on her sample.)

5. Place the light green front panels, flower side up, on top of the 2 dark green back layers, and pin.

6. Stitch the side and bottom edges.

7. Thread the ribbon through the sleeve on the back of the pin saver.

8. With the pin saver face up, slide the ends of the ribbon between the upper side edges of the dark green layers, and pin.

9. Continue stitching along the top edge to catch the ribbon and finish.

Scissor Case
Flower Pattern

Scissor Case
Back Pattern

Scissor Case
Front Pattern

Coffee Cup TOOL CADDY

This incredibly practical (and fast) little swap item will delight your friends! Vicki made her sample from two small pieces of fabric and a coffee mug, but the same principles can be adapted to make caddies out of bigger or smaller containers—widemouthed glasses, mini tin buckets, and more.

Vicki has these wise words of advice about working with your caddy: You will need to adjust the sizes to fit your mug, but this is a place to start. The caddy is basically an outside piece with gussets to hold tools and an inside piece that helps hold the caddy in place. She also used two fabrics for interest and a fusible fleece to add stability.

Made by Vicki Tymczyszyn
Finished size: 4˝ × 11˝

Swap IDEAS

- How about creating a swap around a mug exchange? Give a cute mug with a caddy that is coordinated or themed specifically to the mug. Choose the mug based on what you know about the person.

- In person, you can create a white elephant–type exchange instead of making a mug for a specific person. Everyone brings a funny or interesting mug and caddy, and then they draw numbers. The first person chooses a mug based on the caddy, and the second person either steals the mug from the first, or picks a second mug. If the mug is stolen from the first person, that person then picks another mug. And on it goes. At the end of the game, everyone removes the caddy and enjoys the fun mug hidden underneath.

Vicki began sewing when dinosaurs roamed the earth, or so her children think. She sewed garments for 25 or so years before discovering quilting and has since made way too many to count. (Not that she can't count. It's just that it didn't occur to her when she began that so many people would ask that question.) She likes all needlecraft and has spent countless hours embroidering, cross-stitching, needlepointing, and knitting. She's recently decided to take up crocheting, but that's another story. When she's not working the needles, she's technical editing for *Generation Q Magazine*.

INSTRUCTIONS

All seam allowances are ¼".

1. Fuse the fleece pieces to the matching outer fabric pieces for the inside cylinder, outside flap, and circle following the manufacturer's directions.

2. Sew together the short ends of the 4½" × 10½" outer fabric piece, right sides together, to make a cylinder. Backstitch at both ends.

3. Sew an edge of the cylinder to the outer fabric circle's edge, right sides together. This creates a fabric cup.

4. Sew together the short ends of the 4½" × 10½" lining fabric piece, right sides together, to make a cylinder. Backstitch at both ends.

5. Sew an edge of the cylinder to the lining fabric circle's edge, right sides together. This creates the lining for the fabric cup.

MATERIALS AND SUPPLIES

Outer fabric: ¼ yard

Lining fabric: ¼ yard

Fusible fleece: ¼ yard

CUTTING
WOF = width of fabric

The circle pattern is on page 30. Cut the pattern from tracing paper or template plastic. Measure your mug and adjust the sizes of the pieces as necessary. For the circle, trace the outside bottom of your mug, which will allow for seams.

Outer fabric

Cut 1 strip 4½" × WOF.

Cut strip into:

- 1 rectangle 4½" × 10½" for the inside cylinder.
- 1 rectangle 4½" × 11½" for the outside flap.
- 1 rectangle 3" × 15½" for the pocket.
- 1 circle 3¾" diameter from the pattern.

Lining fabric

Cut 1 strip 4½" × WOF.

Cut strip into:

- 1 rectangle 4½" × 10½" for the inside cylinder.
- 1 rectangle 4½" × 11½" for the outside flap.
- 1 rectangle 3" × 15½" for the pocket.
- 1 circle 3¾" diameter from the pattern.

Fusible fleece

- Cut 1 rectangle 4½" × 10½".
- Cut 1 rectangle 4½" × 11½".
- Cut 1 circle 3¾" diameter from the pattern.

6. Insert the outer fabric cup into the lining cup, wrong sides together. Baste the top edges together.

7. Sew a long edge of the outer fabric and lining fabric pocket pieces, right sides together. Press the seam toward the lining, and then fold and press again with wrong sides together.

8. Fold the pocket piece in half crosswise, and then fold in half again. Press briefly to form folds. Unfold the piece, and use a pin to mark the center fold and the other 2 folds. Repeat with the outer fabric 4½″ × 11½″ flap piece.

9. Place the pocket piece on the flap piece, lining up the ends and fold lines. Stitch on the folds through all the layers. Make pleats at the stitched lines to create 4 pleated pockets.

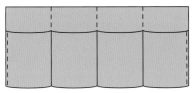

10. Place the 4½″ flap lining piece right sides together over the pocket and outer flap. Stitch along both short ends and the long bottom edge. Trim the corners and turn the piece right side out. Press. Baste the upper edges together.

11. Sew the outer flap with the pocket to the top of the fabric cup, right sides together, and overlap the ends of the outer flap as necessary.

12. Turn the piece right side out and press.

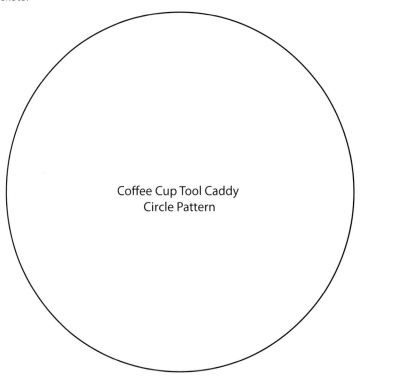

Coffee Cup Tool Caddy
Circle Pattern

Sewing Machine COVER

Lynn says her sewing studio projects here "were inspired by the fantastic quilts of Yoshiko Jinzenji. The negative space of the pale industrial gray contrasts with the rich charcoal containing the dancing colors." The simplicity of the covers' design will give any sewing space a pop of style.

Made by Lynn Kraus

Finished size: Varies

Swap IDEAS

- Pick a room—yes, our favorite is our dream sewing studio—and have participants each make an item for that room. You could put size limits in your rules to prevent a person from giving a quilted tablecloth and receiving a single pot holder.

- Pick an item in a specific room—the sewing machine, the scissors, the ironing board—that the stitcher must accessorize.

- Make it a Twofer Swap, where participants make two related items for each swapee; for instance, add an ironing board cover to the sewing machine cover featured here.

Lynn is a natural-born sewist. As soon as she could hold a needle, she began making clothes for dolls, then for herself. Sewing has always been an integral part of her life. She studied fashion design and apprenticed at a design studio. She lived in Japan, where she studied shibori dyeing. While in Japan, Lynn began quilting. Recently, she has pursued her passion as a fabric rep for E.E. Schenck and as a sales manager for Lecien USA.

MATERIALS AND SUPPLIES

Light gray: 1 yard

Charcoal gray: ½ yard

Bright solid scraps (Charm square packs are great here.)

Batting: craft size

Premade narrow bias tape in gray: 1 package

Basting spray

CUTTING

WOF = width of fabric

Note: Sewing machines are different sizes. The dimensions given are for the machine in the example, a Bernina 180. Measure and note the dimensions of the machine you will be covering.

To allow for ease of getting the cover on and off the machine and a little shrinkage during quilting, add ½˝ to the length and width. The height should be sufficient.

	Project	Yours
Length	14½˝ + ½˝ = 15˝	____ + ½˝ = ____
Width	7½˝ + ½˝ = 8˝	____ + ½˝ = ____
Height	9˝	____

In the example, the height is 9˝ finished. The upper light gray band is 5˝, the pieced band is 3˝, and the bottom charcoal band is 1˝. If your machine is shorter, reduce the width of the upper band. If your machine is taller, increase any of the bands to make up the height.

Gray

- Cut 2 rectangles 5½˝ × 15½˝ for the upper band.
- Cut 2 rectangles 5½˝ × 8½˝ for the sides.
- Cut 2 rectangles 8½˝ × 15½˝ for the top and top lining.
- Cut 2 rectangles 9½˝ × 15½˝ for the front and back lining.
- Cut 2 rectangles 8½˝ × 9½˝ for the side lining.

Charcoal

- Cut 2 strips 1½˝ × WOF for the bottom band.
- Cut 2 strips 2˝ × WOF for the pieced band; then cut them into 5˝ lengths.
- Cut 2 strips 2½˝ × WOF for the binding.

Bright solid scraps

- Randomly cut 1 strip of each color fabric 5˝ × widths that vary from ¾˝ to 1½˝.

Batting

- Cut 1 rectangle 8½˝ × 15½˝ for the top.
- Cut 2 rectangles 9½˝ × 15½˝ for the front and back.
- Cut 2 rectangles 8½˝ × 9½˝ for the sides.

> ### NOTE
> Seventeen fabrics were used in the example. If you have fewer different fabrics, you may wish to cut strips that are longer than 5˝. In this instance, also cut the charcoal strips the same length.

INSTRUCTIONS

All seam allowances are ¼˝.

1. Sew the 5˝ charcoal strips on either side of the bright solid strips. Press toward the charcoal strips. (Although the unfinished width of the pieced band is 3½˝, these strip sets will be wider.) Cut the strip sets into sections at random widths (¾˝ to 2˝) and angles.

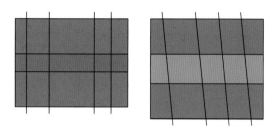

2. Draw 2 horizontal lines 3½˝ apart on a wide piece of paper. Arrange the sections in a pleasing order, with the bright-colored pieces at least ½˝ from either line. Leave a small space between every 4 strips so that you can see the lines on the paper. When you have several arranged as you want, gently lay a ruler over the lines and mark the fabric sections. Use these markings to keep the sections aligned as you sew them together.

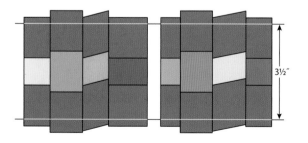

3. Sew the sections together until you have the widths for the front, back, and sides, plus seam allowances. The pieced band is rather stretchy, which makes trimming a little tricky. Smooth out the band and trim to the exact measurements, being careful that it is not too tight or too loose.

4. Sew the pieced bands to the light gray front, back, and side pieces. Press toward the light gray.

5. Sew the top to the front, leaving open ¼˝ at the beginning and end of the seam. Backstitch at both ends. Press the seam open.

6. Sew the front, sides, and back together, leaving open ¼˝ at the top edge of all the seams. Backstitch at the opening. Press the seams open.

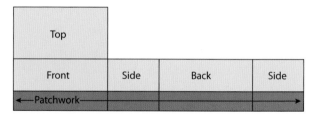

7. Sew the 1½˝ charcoal strips end to end and press. Sew the charcoal strip to the bottom of the pieced band. Trim the excess. Press toward the bottom charcoal band.

Lining

1. Sew the lining pieces the same as the cover. Leave ¼″ open at the top edge of the seams and where the top is sewn to the front. Note that the pieces should be arranged and sewn mirror image to the cover pieces.

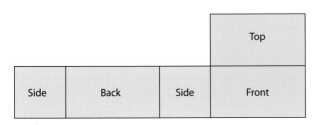

2. Set up a place where you can use the-basting spray adhesive, preferably outside. Read and follow the manufacturer's instructions.

3. Spray the wrong side of the cover. Place it right side down and place the batting pieces on it, preferably under the seam allowances if possible. Smooth to assure good adhesion.

4. Spray the wrong side of the lining. Matching the front and top seams first, smooth the rest of the lining onto the batting.

5. Using an erasable marker, mark the upper light gray sections ¼″ from the pieced band seam. Then mark every ½″.

6. On the top piece, mark ¼″ from the top/front seam; then mark every ½″.

7. Quilt every line, going in opposite directions.

8. Stitch in-the-ditch in both pieced band seams.

9. Quilt the charcoal band ¼″ from the seam, then another line ¼″ from the first. Remove the markings and press well.

10. Sew the side to the front, being particularly careful to match the pieced band seams.

11. Match the top to the back and sew. The ¼″ openings in the seam allowances should make this easier.

12. Match and sew the side pieces to the top piece. This may require a little adjustment of the seam allowances at the corners.

13. Use the purchased bias tape to cover the raw seams inside.

14. Sew the binding strips together with diagonal seams. Trim the seam allowance ¼″ and press open. Press in half lengthwise, with the wrong sides together.

15. With raw edges even, pin and sew the binding to the cover. Overlap or seam the ends.

16. Bring the folded edge to the inside and stitch it in place.

17. Press well, including the side and top seams, to create sharp edges and corners.

Hot Drink POUCHES

Quick and easy is always a great way to swap, and these pouches are the answer. Stitch these up in less than an hour, and you're set. The coffee version has narrow pockets for those tubes of instant coffee or water drinks. The tea version has a bigger pouch for tea bags.

Made by Vicki Tymczyszyn

Finished size: 3½˝ × 5˝

- Tons of food and drink projects can be adapted for a great swap. Consider the simple theme of hot drinks—coffee, tea—and you've probably covered everyone playing. Add on a hot dish and suddenly you're making always-at-hand pot holders and casserole covers. Other things to make that are hot: mug rug, cup holder, place mats, and so on.

- Make it easy. The swap theme is fast and fun! It has to be done in an hour or less.

MATERIALS AND SUPPLIES

Prints for outer fabric, lining, and pocket:
¼ yard each or scraps

Fusible batting: ⅛ yard

Hook-and-loop tape

CUTTING

Prints

- Cut 1 rectangle 4″ × 10″ for the outer pouch.
- Cut 1 rectangle 4″ × 10″ for the lining.
- Cut 1 square 6½″ × 6½″ for the pocket.

Fusible batting

- Cut 1 rectangle 4″ × 10″.

INSTRUCTIONS

All seam allowances are ¼″.

1. Following the manufacturer's directions, fuse the batting to the wrong side of the lining.

2. Fold the pocket in half, wrong sides together, and press.

3. Place the pocket piece on top of the lining, right side up. Align the sides of both pieces, and baste them together.

4. For the tea pouch, form pleats at the side edges of the pocket. For the coffee pouch, stitch in the center of the pocket, from the folded edge to the bottom. Form pleats at the stitching and at the sides to create 2 gusseted pockets. Press the gussets into place.

5. Sew the outer fabric to the lining/pocket piece, right sides together, leaving an opening in the short end opposite the pockets for turning. Trim the corners and turn right side out. Press.

6. Turn the seam at the open end to the inside, and topstitch it closed. Add hook-and-loop tape to the appropriate spots to close the pouch.

Artist: Vicki Tymczyszyn
Meet this artist on page 28.

French Pressed for Pleasure COVER

Why not plunge into something a little different? How about dressing up a French press? Besides adding a splash of color, this cover will also keep the heat in, giving you just a little longer to savor the java.

Made by Vicki Tymczyszyn

Finished size: Varies

Swap IDEA

This is a great in-person swap because these covers need to be made specifically for each French press. So have participants bring the French press they want to cover. Online, the French press dimensions would obviously have to be part of the get-to-know-you questions. Measure twice, write once. Take first responsibility in making the cover the right size.

Considering an extra for the gift package? Add a favorite coffee—bagged for the press of course!

MATERIALS AND SUPPLIES

Outer fabric: fat quarter

Lining: fat quarter

Insulated interfacing, such as Insul-Fleece by C&T Publishing: ¼ yard

1″ hook-and-loop tape: ¼ yard

CUTTING

These measurements are for the pictured French press. Measure your pot and adjust accordingly.

Outer fabric and lining

- Cut 1 rectangle 7½″ × 14½″ from each.

- Cut 2 rectangles 2″ × 3″ for the tabs.

Insul-Fleece

- Cut 1 rectangle 7½″ × 14½″.

Artist: Vicki Tymczyszyn
Meet this artist on page 28.

INSTRUCTIONS

All seam allowances are ¼˝.

1. Wrap the lining fabric around the coffee press, and mark any handles; cut a notch in the fabric, allowing for seams.

Vicki's French press required a 1˝ × 1½˝ notch approximately 2˝ down from the cover top.

2. Sew a side of the hook-and-loop tape to the 2˝ × 3˝ lining tabs. Pair with the outer fabric tabs, right sides together, and sew around the edges, leaving a short end open to turn the piece right side out. Trim the corners and turn right side out. Press.

3. Place the tabs on a short end of the outer fabric, approximately 1˝ from the top edge and ½˝ from the bottom edge, and baste them in place.

4. Fuse Insul-Fleece to the lining fabric with the metallic side toward the lining.

5. Sew the outer fabric to the lining, right sides together, following the contours of any notches and leaving a 3˝ opening for turning along the bottom edge. Trim the corners and turn right side out; press.

6. Press the opening and topstitch it closed. Topstitch all the edges.

7. Wrap the coffee press with the cover, and mark for the hook-and-loop placement. Add the other side of the hook-and-loop tape to the cover.

Tea Cozy & MAT

Is there anything better than sitting with your favorite people and sharing a pot of tea or coffee? Uh, no! So we're encouraging you to take that time and enjoy someone else's company with Karen's pretty little cozy. We worked with a standard teapot, but you can easily adapt the cover.

Made by Karen Cunagin

Finished sizes:

Teapot Cover: 9˝ × 14˝

Mat: 9˝ × 14˝

Artist: Karen Cunagin
Website: karencunagin.com

Swap IDEA

What if everyone participating in the swap takes a picture of his or her teapot? Participants draw a picture instead of a name, and then make a cozy-mat combo to suit the pot! Tea cozies and mats are easily personalized by fabric choices and added elements, such as a tea bag pocket or beaded loops. Matching the pot to the owner at the reveal makes this a blast.

Karen teaches college classes in artful quilting in San Diego and loves speaking to guilds and sharing her quilts in live presentations. She was nominated for the Teacher of the Year award 2011 by *The Professional Quilter* magazine. Her work has been shown in *Visions: The Art Quilt 2006*, regional juried shows, and international publications. Both machine sewn and hand stitched, her works of art revolve around themes of the intimate world of family, the garden, and spiritual work.

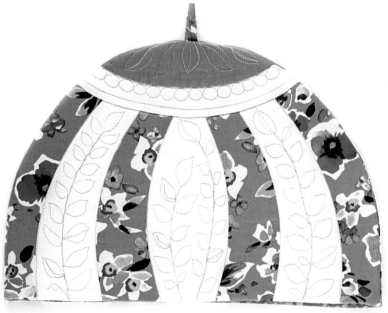

MATERIALS AND SUPPLIES

White fabric: ½ yard

Blue fabric: fat quarter

Pink fabric: ⅛ yard

Lining and binding: 1 yard

Insul-Fleece insulated interfacing: craft pack or ½ yard

Tracing paper or template plastic

Permanent fine-line marker

Basting spray

CUTTING

The patterns are on pages 46–50. Trace and cut each pattern piece from tracing paper or template plastic.

White

- Cut 2 A on the fold for the cover.

- Cut 2 C and 2 C reversed for the cover.

- Cut 2 F for the cover.

- Cut 1 G, H, I, J, and K for the mat.

Blue

- Cut 2 B and 2 B reversed for the cover.

- Cut 2 D and 2 D reversed for the cover.

- Cut 1 strip 1″ × 4½″ on the bias for the cover loop.

- Cut 1 G, H, I, J, and K for the mat.

Pink

- Cut 2 E for the cover.

- Cut 2 L for the mat.

Binding

- Cut 1 strip 1½″ × 35″ on the bias for the cover binding.

- Cut 1 strip 1½″ × 45″ on the bias for the mat binding.

INSTRUCTIONS

All seam allowances are ¼˝.

Cover Assembly

1. Arrange the cover pieces as shown.

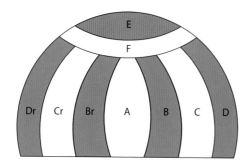

2. To easily piece curved seams, fold the pieces in half lengthwise, and make a small crease. With right sides together, pin the edges together from the crease to the ends. By using many pins, you won't need to clip. Sew the seams and then press toward the darker fabric.

3. For each side of the cover, crease and pin B reverse to A, C to D, and C reverse to D reverse. Press all seams toward the darker fabric.

4. Repeat creasing and pinning to sew C/D to B and C reverse/D reverse to B reverse. Press all seams toward the darker fabric.

5. Repeat creasing and pinning to sew E to F. Then sew E/F to the cover's A/B/C/D bottom section. Press the seam toward E/F.

6. Layer the lining, right side down, and Insul-Fleece together. Place each cover side on the Insul-Fleece, trace the outline, and cut the layers out. Spray baste the layers together. Baste stitch ⅛˝ from the edges.

7. Quilt the cover pieces as desired.

8. To make the loop, fold the 1˝ × 4½˝ piece lengthwise, right sides together. Sew ¼˝ along the long edge. Turn the tube right side out using a small safety pin or loop turner. Press. Fold the loop in half. Pin the edges of the loop to the top center of a side of the cover, matching raw edges. Stitch in place ⅛˝ from the edge.

9. Layer the 2 sides of the cover right sides together, and pin along the rounded edges. Sew together. Finish the raw edges with a zigzag stitch, or stitch by hand.

10. Press the binding strip in half lengthwise, with wrong sides together. With raw edges even, pin and sew the binding to the cover. Overlap or seam the ends. Turn the binding and the seam allowance to the inside, and stitch in place.

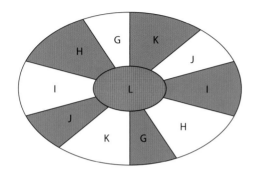

Mat Assembly

1. Arrange mat pieces as shown.

2. Sew the wedges together in a circle, pressing the seams toward the darker fabric.

3. Layer the lining, right side down, and Insul-Fleece together. Lay the pieced mat on the Insul-Fleece, trace the outline, and cut out the layers. Spray baste the layers together. Baste stitch ⅛″ from the edge.

4. Quilt as desired.

5. With right sides together, sew the L pieces together along the outside edges. Carefully clip along the curves. Make a small cut in the center of a side, and turn the piece right side out. Press to smooth the curves.

6. Lay the L piece on the center of the oval mat with the cut side down. Sew it in place just along the inside edge.

7. Press the binding strip in half lengthwise, with the wrong sides together. With raw edges even, pin and sew the binding to the mat. Overlap or seam the ends. Turn the binding and the seam allowance to the back, and stitch in place.

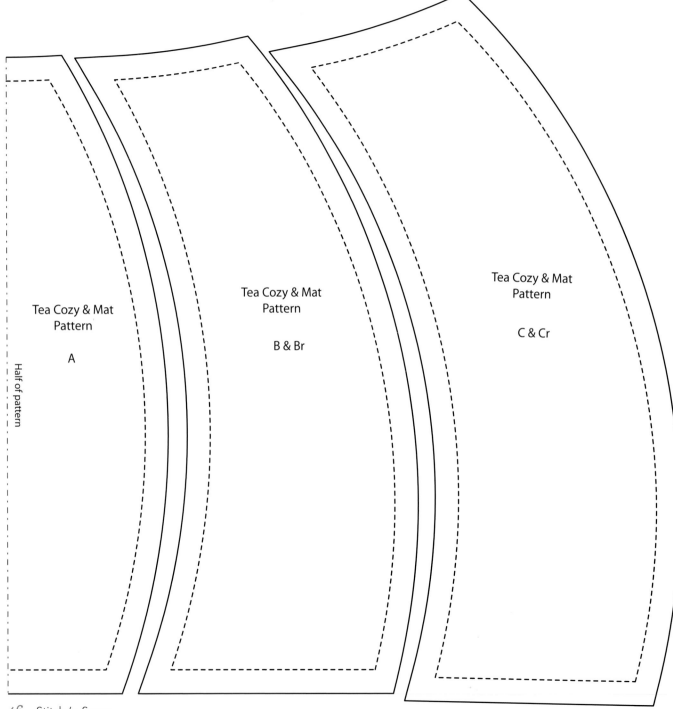

Tea Cozy & Mat
Pattern

A

Half of pattern

Tea Cozy & Mat
Pattern

B & Br

Tea Cozy & Mat
Pattern

C & Cr

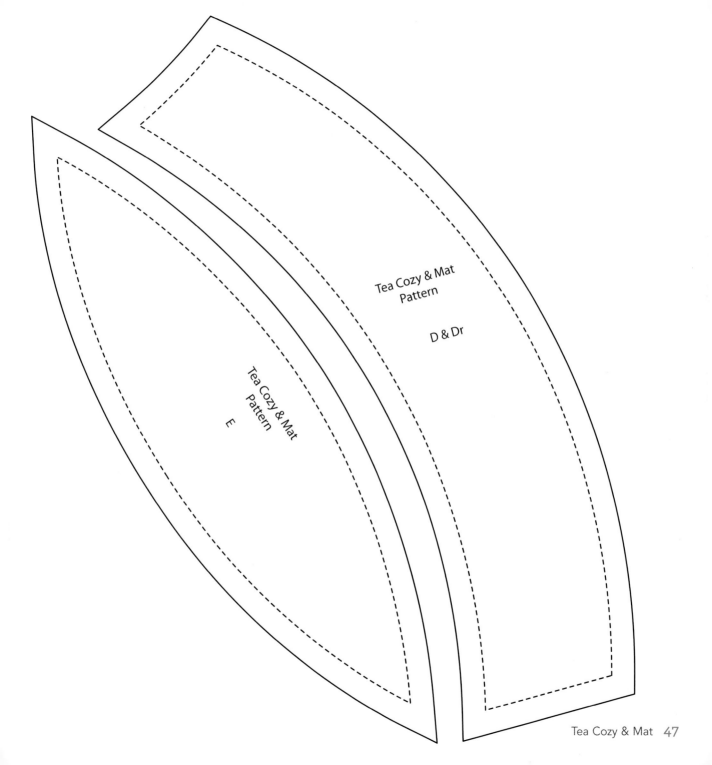

Tea Cozy & Mat
Pattern

D & Dr

Tea Cozy & Mat
Pattern

E

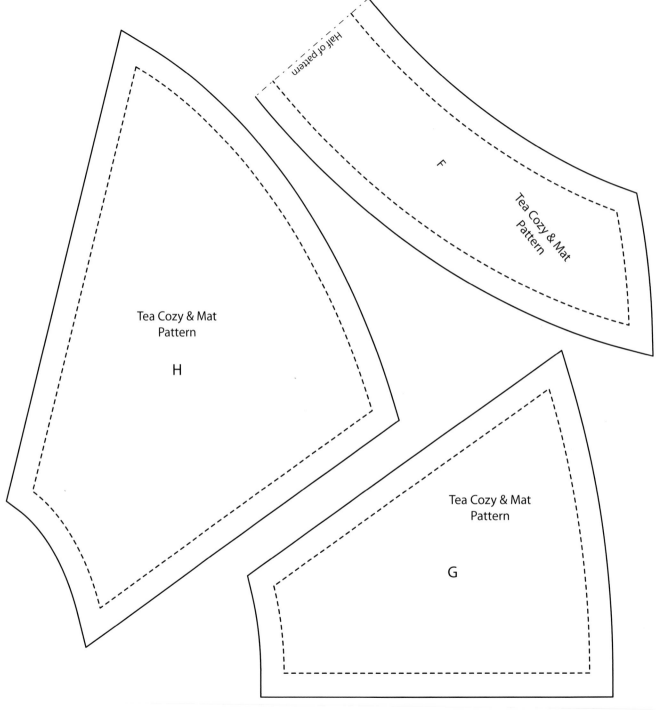

Half of pattern

F

Tea Cozy & Mat
Pattern

Tea Cozy & Mat
Pattern

H

Tea Cozy & Mat
Pattern

G

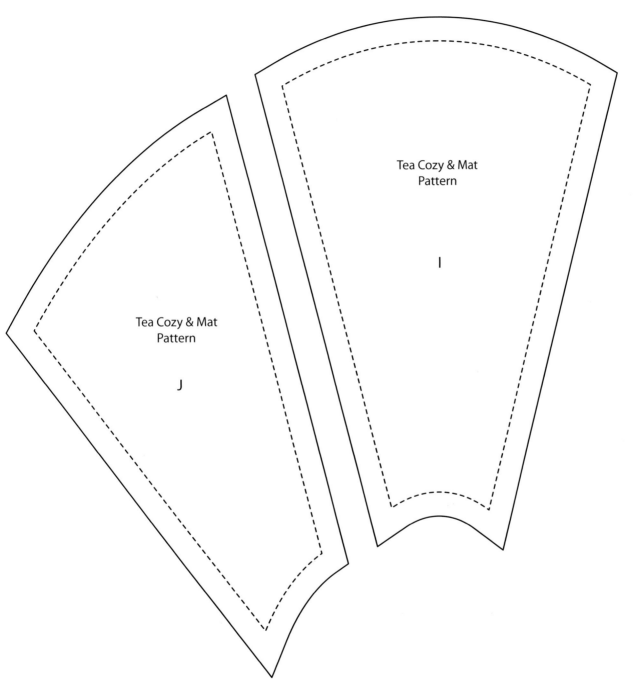

Tea Cozy & Mat
Pattern

I

Tea Cozy & Mat
Pattern

J

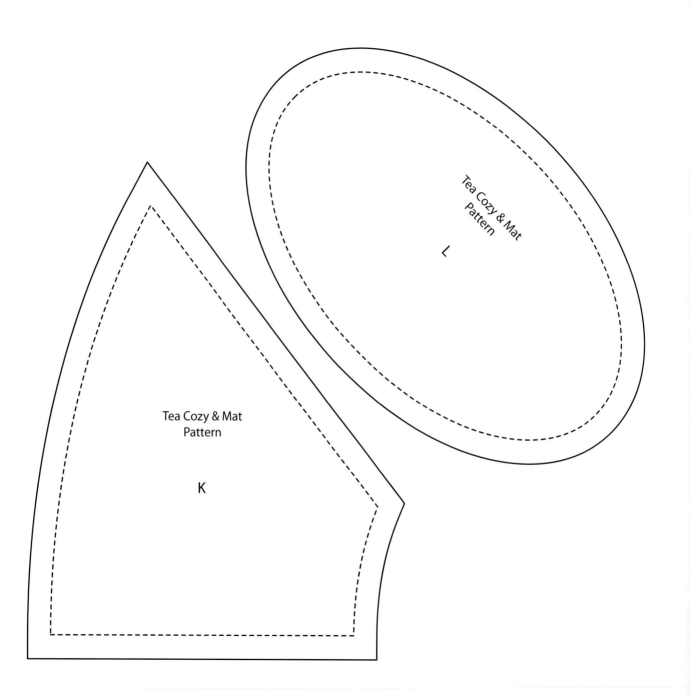

Tea Cozy & Mat
Pattern

L

Tea Cozy & Mat
Pattern

K

Parquet POT HOLDERS

Made by Kevin Kosbab

Pot holders come in many styles and shapes these days, and most of them are very simple to make. A pot holder consists of fabric and heat-resistant batting, such as Insul-Fleece. The biggest consideration when making pot holders is that they should be washable and have no dangling features (loops for hanging don't count). Made from a classic Rail Fence block, Kevin's pot holders come in two versions, a pinwheel setting and a chevron pattern. They are super simple to make, pretty, and useful.

Finished size: 8½˝ × 8½˝, not including hanging loop

Artist: Kevin Kosbab
Website: feeddog.net
Blog: feeddog.blogspot.com

Swap IDEA

Build a swap around a classic quilt block. Each player has to use the classic block in two variations to make two pot holders for the recipient. Whether the whole group uses the same block design or everyone uses a different one is up to the group. But it will increase the challenge if each person has to blindly choose or is assigned a classic block.

Kevin designs quilting and sewing patterns for a variety of publications as well as his own pattern line, Feed Dog Designs. He loves bright colors, bold graphics, and smart designs. His DVD, *Secrets of Home Décor Sewing,* is available now, and his first quilting book will be released in early 2014. Currently residing in northern California, he also works as a freelance writer and editor.

MATERIALS AND SUPPLIES

Makes 1

Note: If you're working with multiple fabrics, have additional strips on hand, each 1½˝ wide. Each piece of the block measures 1½˝ × 2½˝ (1˝ × 2˝ finished). If you're using more fabrics, find the length of the strips by multiplying the number of pieces needed by 2½˝; then sew in the same way.

Solid red fabric: 1 strip 1½˝ × WOF

Striped fabric: 1 strip 1½˝ × WOF

Backing fabric: 9˝ × 9˝ square

Batting or insulated interfacing, such as Insul-Fleece by C&T Publishing: 9˝ × 9˝ square

Binding: 1 strip 2˝ × WOF   *WOF = width of fabric*

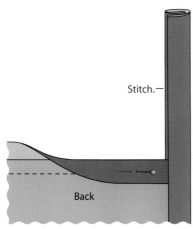

Stitch.

Back

INSTRUCTIONS

All seam allowances are ¼″.

1. Plan your design: the chevron and pinwheel designs shown here are just a couple of examples of different patterns that can be made with the same basic block.

2. Sew the strips right sides together along a long edge. Press the seams to the side, and then cut the strip set into 2½″ sections. Arrange the sections into 4 rows of 4, alternating horizontal and vertical seam placement to create your intended design.

3. Sew the squares together in rows or in Four-Patch units, depending on your design. Press the seams to the side, and then join the rows or Four-Patch units to complete the block.

4. Layer the backing, wrong side up, with the batting and block, right side up. Baste. Then quilt as desired. The pinwheel sample was stitched in-the-ditch along all the seams, while channels were quilted parallel to the aqua zigzags to help bring out the chevron pattern. Trim away the excess batting and backing, and square up the pot holder.

5. Press the binding strip in half lengthwise, wrong sides together. Starting at the corner where you want to place the hanging loop, align the raw edges and sew the binding to all the layers. Stop a few inches from the starting corner when you near the end.

6. Trim the excess binding, leaving a 4″ tail to create the hanging loop. With the raw edges of the binding together, press under ¼″. Bring the folded edge of the beginning end of the binding to the back and pin. Wrap the tail end of the binding over the edge of the pot holder, enclosing the beginning end of the binding. Hand stitch or topstitch to finish attaching the binding and close the open edge of the tail.

7. Fold the tail to form a loop, and tuck the end under the folded beginning edge of the binding. Topstitch or hand sew the binding to the back, stitching the hanging loop so it lies flat.

Mini Casserole CARRIER

Sometimes you don't need to haul a big, complicated carrier made for a big 9˝ × 13˝ hot dish. Reach for this wee one when you're toting a small hot (or cold) dish. Perfectly sized for an 8˝ square or round casserole, or a 1½- to 2-quart dish, it's fully washable, and the serving spoon helps hold it closed.

(Bonus: Great project for practicing your quilting skills!)

Made by Melissa Thompson Maher

Finished size: 14˝ × 16˝

Swap IDEAS

- In person, you can turn your reveal into a potluck! Put your work to work; bring in your casserole cover with a food-filled dish. For the exchange, provide the recipe for the dish in your cover. Drop the recipe in a bag (or hat, whatever) and draw. Find the dish that matches the recipe you pick; that's your new casserole cover!

- Online swappers are going to want a recipe, too. Each participant can supply a recipe, which would then be used instead of names or numbers to swap covers. You get the carrier made by the person whose recipe you were given.

- Or if you have that super-organized, ready-to-take-on-every-new-project facilitator, participants could each list just the ingredients of a recipe they want to share; then—not knowing what the recipe will actually make—people choose the list that's the most appealing to them. The facilitator makes sure each recipe is only given out once! In the reveal, you get the complete recipe from the swapee and the casserole carrier he or she made.

- After the online or in-person reveal, compile the recipes and share them all with the entire group.

Melissa is the *Generation Q Magazine* co-founder and editor-in-chief. She has been sewing and reporting on textile arts for a long time. (Let's leave it at that.) She loves fabric, and when her schedule is too jammed for sew-time, she's been known to fondle her stash for a little mood enhancement. She also loves hand and machine embroidery. Before joining the quilting/sewing industry, she pioneered coverage on the commercial embroidery industry with *Stitches Magazine*. (But *GenQ* is more fun.)

MATERIALS AND SUPPLIES

Green print: ½ yard for outer fabric

Orange print: ½ yard for lining

Insulated interfacing, such as Insul-Fleece by C&T Publishing: ½ yard

Solid green: ½ yard for straps, binding, and loops

Lightweight fusible interfacing: ⅝ yard

Wooden spoon

TIP

The basic pattern size is 12˝ × 14˝. If you'd like the pattern to accommodate a 9˝ square or round dish, enlarge it 2˝–3˝ along the long sides and 1˝–2˝ on the short sides. Measure the perimeter of the finished carrier before cutting the bias binding to make sure you cut enough.

INSTRUCTIONS

All seam allowances are ¼˝.

Carrier

The pattern for the corners is on page 58. Trace and cut the pattern piece from tracing paper or template plastic.

1. Layer the lining fabric, wrong side up, with the Insul-Fleece and outer fabric, right side up. Repeat with the second set.

2. Quilt each sandwich as desired.

3. Use the pattern to trim the corners from the pieces.

4. Fold a piece crosswise, and finger-press the fold. Cut on the fold to make 2 halves. This will become the carrier's top. Along the cut line of each half, trim ⅛˝ from the edge. This will create a slight gap when the carrier is finished to provide ease for inserting and removing the dish.

5. Trim 2 pieces of binding 14˝ long. Fold and press them in half lengthwise. Sew them to the trimmed edges of each half of the carrier's top. Bring the binding to the lining side, and sew it in place by hand or machine.

CUTTING

Green print

- Cut 2 rectangles 14″ × 16″.

Orange print

- Cut 2 rectangles 14″ × 16″.

Insul-Fleece

- Cut 2 rectangles 14″ × 16″.

Solid green

- Cut 1 strip 4½″ × WOF; trim to 40″ long for the straps.

- Cut 6 strips 2½″ on the bias of the fabric for the binding.

- Cut 1 rectangle 2½″ × 4″ and 1 rectangle 2½″ × 10″ for the loops.

Lightweight fusible interfacing

- Cut 2 strips 4″ × 20″ for the straps.

- Cut 1 rectangle 2″ × 4″ and 1 rectangle 2″ × 10″ for the loops.

WOF = width of fabric

Closures

1. Fold and press the 2½″ × 4″ and 2½″ × 10″ loop pieces in half lengthwise, wrong sides together. Open each piece and fuse the corresponding interfacing pieces to the wrong side of the loop pieces. Fold under ¼″ on the long edges and press. Refold the pieces along the original center fold and press. Topstitch along both long edges. At the ends of each piece, fold under ½″ and press.

2. Mark the center of the bound edge of each half of the carrier's top.

3. For the 10″ loop, pin the folded ends 2″ from the bound edge on either side of the center mark. Sew in place on the ends and again next to the binding.

TIP

Melissa used a tight zigzag stitch on the loops for extra strength.

4. For the 4″ loop, pin and sew the folded end 2″ from the bound edge on the center mark of the carrier's other top piece. Pin and sew the other end next to the binding to create a hump.

Straps

1. Place the interfacing on the wrong side of the strap piece, ¼″ away from the long edges, and fuse following the manufacturer's directions.

2. Fold over both raw edges ¼″, and press them in place. Then fold the strip in half, wrong sides together, and press the fold in place. Topstitch both edges to hold them together. Cut the strip in half to make 2 straps 20″ long.

3. Place the carrier bottom lining side up. Layer the 2 carrier top pieces right side up. Baste the pieces together ⅛″ from the edges.

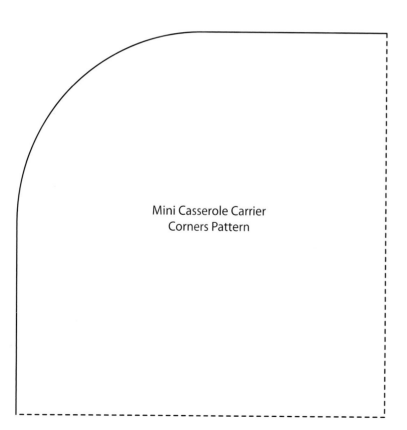

Mini Casserole Carrier
Corners Pattern

4. With the bottom side up, mark the center of the carrier's short ends. Measure 1½″ from both sides of the mark, and pin. Place the ends of the straps at the pins, with the straps facing in. Baste in place.

5. Sew the binding strips together with diagonal seams. Press open. Press in half lengthwise with wrong sides together.

6. With the bottom side of the carrier up, sew the binding to the outside edges of the carrier. Press the binding over the seam allowance, then over to the carrier top, and hand or machine stitch it in place.

7. Insert the spoon through the loop closure.

Diaper CLUTCH

Any new parent can appreciate this handy diaper clutch that holds all of baby's quick-change essentials. With a built-in mat and pockets for diapers and wipes, you're all set. Now it's likely this project won't suit the needs of every swap participant in a group; check out the swap idea.

Finished sizes:

Open: 29″ × 36″

Closed: 7″ × 11″

Made by Elaine Wong Haselhuhn

Artist: Elaine Wong Haselhuhn
Blog: dashasel.blogspot.com

Swap IDEA

Here is a pattern with a very specific purpose, but if you don't have a need for a diaper clutch in your group, how can you repurpose this project? Cosmetic case? Traveling chalkboard? How about a craft tote? If you traded the inner fabric for flannel and tailored the pocket dividers to smaller sizes, it could transport embroidery projects. The project can be folded on the flannel side, and scissors, floss, hoop, and other tools can be held in the pockets. Have your participants stretch their design muscles through adaptation. (Unless they happen to be partnered with a new parent, in which case they totally lucked out!)

Whether it is sewing, pottery, knitting, or metalsmithing, if you name a craft, it is likely that Elaine has tried it (and has the stash to show for it!). Though some crafts have come and gone, sewing remains one of Elaine's favorites. Elaine started to sew in 2009, when she was expecting a baby. She started with a simple baby blanket, joined a few quilting bees, and hasn't stopped since!

MATERIALS AND SUPPLIES

Laminated cotton for outer clutch and pockets: 1½ yards

Laminated cotton for clutch lining: 1 yard

Contrasting fabric: ½ yard for binding or packaged commercial binding

¾˝ hook-and-loop tape: 1¾ yards (*Stick-on is recommended, but the nonstick version is okay if you are using cotton.*)

¾˝ fold-over elastic: ½ yard (*Regular elastic is okay but not as stretchy.*)

Decorative button

Hera marker*

Walking foot*

Clover Wonder Clips*

* These items make working with laminates much easier.

CUTTING

Outer fabric
- Cut 1 rectangle 29˝ × 36˝ for the outer clutch.
- Cut 1 rectangle 19˝ × 29˝ for the pockets.

Lining fabric
- Cut 1 rectangle 29˝ × 36˝ for the clutch lining.

Binding
- Cut 6 strips 2½˝ on the bias of the fabric.

INSTRUCTIONS

All seam allowances are ¼˝. The pattern for the flap is on page 63. Trace the pattern on tracing paper or template plastic.

1. On the right side of the outer fabric, measure 7˝ from the end along both 36˝ edges. With a Hera marker or chalk pencil, connect the marks.

2. Measure and mark along the marked line 6½˝ from an edge and 11½˝ from the other edge.

3. Trace the flap pattern between the above marks. Trim the edge on the marked lines.

4. Place the trimmed outer fabric right side up on the wrong side of the lining fabric. Pin or Wonder Clip along the edges, and trim the lining to match the outer fabric piece.

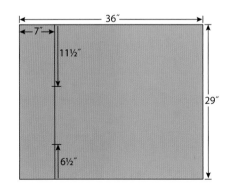

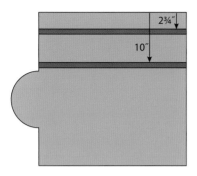

5. On the right side of the lining piece, on the 11½" side of the flap, mark lines parallel to the 36" side, the first 2¾" from the edge and the other 10" from the edge. Sew the hook-and-loop tape next to these lines.

TIP

Using sticky-backed hook-and-loop tape works better because pinning on laminated cotton is hard.

Pockets

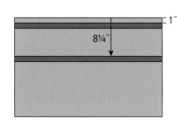

1. On the right side of the pocket piece, mark lines parallel to the 29" side, the first 1" from the edge and the other 8¼" from the edge. Sew the hook-and-loop tape next to these lines.

2. Fold the pocket piece in half lengthwise with right sides together. Sew to create a long tube. Finger-press the seam open. Turn the tube right side out and finger-press. Topstitch both long edges of the flattened tube.

3. Place the pocket on top of the lining, adhering the hook-and-loop tapes. Mark the desired pocket sizes. The pockets on the sample are at intervals of 2½", 6½", 6½", 8", and 4½". Sew on the lines. Backstitch for added strength. The hook-and-loop tape keeps the contents of the pockets secure and allows access from either side.

Assembly

1. Layer the outer clutch fabric with the lining, wrong sides together. Use Wonder Clips to hold the pieces together. Baste ⅛" from the edges.

2. Mark and stitch lines from each side of the flap to the opposite edge. The first line of stitching will be 6½" from the edge; the other will be just below the pocket piece.

3. Fold the piece of elastic in half. Baste the ends in place on the outer fabric at the center of the flap, with raw edges together.

4. Sew the binding strips end to end with diagonal seams. Press in half lengthwise with the wrong sides together.

5. With the raw edges even, pin and sew the binding to the clutch, catching the elastic ends. Overlap or seam the ends. Bring the binding to the lining, and hand stitch it in place. If you're using commercial binding, attach it with a zigzag stitch.

....

TIP

Use a zigzag stitch to sew the binding down.

....

6. Add a button to help secure the elastic.

7. To close the clutch, fold the pocket edge over to the center; then fold the other long edge to the center. Fold the end to the flap, and then fold again. Use the elastic to close the clutch.

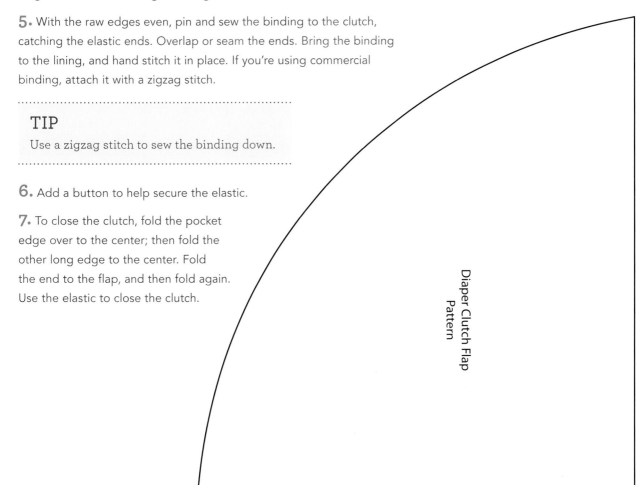

Diaper Clutch Flap Pattern

Half of pattern

Chillax EYE PILLOWS

These super-easy, scrappy, collage-y, reversible lavender-flower eye pillows are fun and addictive to make. Put them in the freezer to be ready when your eyes are puffy; keep one in your yoga bag or next to the bed. The little tags add just the right touch of cute!

Made by Carrie Bloomston
Finished size: 4˝ × 9¼˝

Artist: Carrie Bloomston
Website: such-designs.com

Swap IDEAS

- In person: Consider a Spa Swap among a small group of friends where the reveal happens at a local spa, or even a nail salon. Bring your eye pillows with you. Each pillow's design can be easily tailored to your swapee, as can the pillow's scented contents.

- Online: Use a spa or bath theme. Have everyone do an eye pillow plus another spa-perfect gift. An embroidered towel? A neck pillow? A fabric tray or basket liner? Then, of course, soaps, lotions, or candles are the perfect extra.

- Make your swap a Multiuse Swap. Whatever you make has to have more than one use. These eye pillows, for instance, could be cold/hot packs or dresser drawer sachets!

Carrie expresses herself through art, and design allows her to share the joy and awe she feels. Her work—whether abstract painting, designing sewing patterns and fabric, or parenting—is all about expressing joy and love. She sees art as a place to figure the world out, to make sense of it. She says, "Think of me as your inner-artist enabler. I want to help you celebrate your inner artist, too."

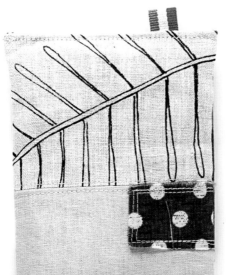

Collage Style

1. Cut the top rectangle 4½″ × 7″.

2. Cut a contrasting piece 4½″ × 3¼″. Pin the 4½″ edges right sides together and sew. Press the seams open. Topstitch on each side of the seam.

3. Cut small rectangles of scraps to create a collaged look. Use a washable school gluestick to stick them down. Sew over each scrap in an artful, overlapping way as pictured.

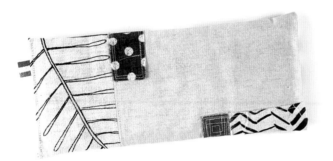

Pieced Style

1. Cut the top rectangle 4½″ × 8″.

2. Cut a contrasting piece 4½″ × 2¼″. Pin the 4½″ edges right sides together and sew. Press the seams open.

Embroidered Style

Use a simple computer font to write your sentiment. Trace on the fabric using a lightbox.

1. Cut the top rectangle 6″ × 12″.

2. Use an embroidery hoop for stability, 4 strands of floss, and a running stitch to embroider the words.

3. Trim the rectangle to 4½″ × 9¾″.

FINISHING EACH PILLOW

1. Cut a rectangle 4½″ × 9¾″ for each back.

2. With the top's wrong side facing up, fold a short edge over a generous ¼″ and press. Repeat with the matching edge on the back piece. Place the top and back right sides together.

3. Sew along the other 3 sides, backstitching at the start and end. Trim the threads and clip the corners. Turn the eye pillow right side out, and use a dull pencil to gently push out the corners. Press.

4. Fill the pillow with 1¾ cups of equal parts lavender flowers and rice. You can add dried herbs or flowers, but if they are too large, crush them so they won't poke through the fabric.

5. Cut a 2″ piece of twill tape or ribbon, fold it in half, and press. Insert the ends of the ribbon between the turned-under ends, and topstitch to close the pillow.

MATERIALS AND SUPPLIES

Cotton and linen fabric scraps: 5″ × 7″ to 6″ × 12″ (about ½ yard total for all 3 pillows)

Ribbon or twill tape

Washable school gluestick

2–4 ounces lavender flowers (available at health food stores)

White rice (for weight and bulk)

Embroidery hoop

Cotton embroidery floss

Embroidery needle

Carrie made 3 different eye pillows, but the construction is the same for each. We're providing the instructions for each top first and then the overall instructions for finishing the pillows. All seam allowances are ¼″.

Baggin' It GROCERY TOTE

Having grocery totes on hand helps care for the planet. Recycling does, too. This project is a perfect start to recycling and reusing. Emily designed this bag with an inset for a 12˝ finished quilt block. While she came up with a great paper-pieced block pattern of the recycle symbol, feel free to switch out this area for any 12˝ finished block you want.

Made by Emily Herrick

Finished size: 14˝ wide × 15˝ high × 6˝ deep

Swap IDEAS

- Hold a swap that benefits the community as well as your swapees. Each participant draws a name and makes a super-personal grocery tote bag for his or her swapee. For the reveal, the bag is stuffed with canned and dry goods, which are then donated to a local food bank. You get to feel good in more ways than one!

- Online, send the bag to your swapee along with a picture of the items you're donating to your local food bank.

- For more open-ended swaps, based on a fabric or technique for instance, bags are great go-to projects. If the theme is handles, zippers, or embellishments, again, go to the bags!

Emily began her creative journey at a young age, drawing on her bedroom walls. Thankfully, her talent has taken a much more productive turn in the form of quilt patterns (Crazy Old Ladies), fabric designs (licensed with Michael Miller Fabrics), and writing a book (she released her first self-published book, *Geared for Guys*, in 2012). Emily lives in Utah with her husband, Gilbert, and their children, Preston, Logan, and Paris.

INSTRUCTIONS

Seam allowances are ¼″ except where noted. These instructions include a 12″ finished block. The block's instructions follow (page 72).

1. Sew the 4½″ × 12½″ outer fabric rectangles to the sides of the 12½″ quilt block. Press the seams away from the block.

2. Sew the 2″ × 20½″ outer fabric rectangle to the top of the block. Press the seam away from the block.

3. Sew the 21″ × 22½″ outer fabric rectangle to the bottom of the block. Press the seam away from the block. This large piece forms the lower front, the bottom, and the back of the tote.

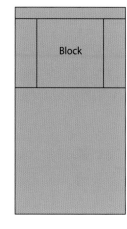

4. Fuse the 20″ × 36″ piece of interfacing to the wrong side of the tote following the manufacturer's directions.

5. Topstitch outside the edge of the quilt block.

MATERIALS AND SUPPLIES

Outer fabric: 1 yard for bag and block pieces

Lining fabric: ¾ yard of laminated cotton

Scraps for paper-pieced block and handles

Lightweight fusible interfacing: 1½ yards

CUTTING

Outer fabric

- Cut 2 rectangles 4½″ × 12½″ for the bag.
- Cut 1 rectangle 2″ × 21″ for the bag.
- Cut 1 rectangle 21″ × 22½″ for the bag.
- Cut 1 rectangle 2½″ × 6½″ for the block.
- Cut 2 rectangles 3½″ × 6½″ for the block.

Lining fabric

- Cut 1 rectangle 21″ × 36″ for the lining.

Lightweight fusible interfacing

- Cut 1 rectangle 20″ × 36″.
- Cut 2 strips 4″ × 26″.

6. Fold the tote in half crosswise, right sides together. Sew ½″ seams on both side edges. Press the seams open. Then topstitch along each side of the seams.

NOTE

Sew as far as possible toward the fold, but don't worry if you can't reach the very bottom. The ends of the seams won't be seen after the bag is squared up.

7. Turn the tote wrong side out. Create box corners on the tote's bottom by folding the tote at a corner, matching up the side seam and bottom fold to make a triangle. Use a ruler to find where the point measures 5½″ across. Mark this line with a pencil or pen. Then sew over this line 2 or 3 times. Trim the seam to ½″. Repeat with the other corner.

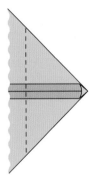

8. Turn the bag right side out.

Lining and Handles

1. Fold the lining piece in half crosswise. Repeat Steps 6 and 7 above. Leave the lining inside out.

2. Piece scraps together to create 2 strips 4″ × 26″.

3. Center the interfacing on the wrong side of each pieced strip, and fuse it in place.

4. Fold the strips in half lengthwise, wrong sides together, and press. Open and fold the side edges to the middle fold and press. Then fold them in half and press again. Sew 5 lines of topstitching on each handle for stability.

FINISHING

1. On the right side of the tote's top edge, mark 6″ in from the side seams to make 4 marks total. Pin each end of the handles on a mark. Zigzag stitch them in place for stability.

2. Tuck the bag, handles down, into the lining. The right sides will face together. Pin the top edges of the bag and lining together, making sure to line up the side seams.

3. Sew a 1″ seam around the tote's edge, leaving about a 6″ opening. Carefully turn the bag right side out. Fold in the seam allowances at the opening, and topstitch close to the edge. Sew a second line of stitching ¾″ from the top edge.

RECYCLING BLOCK PAPER-PIECING INSTRUCTIONS

The block has 3 smaller blocks, with 2 sections (A and B) for each block. The patterns are on pages 73–75. Photocopy 2 copies of each block from the same copy machine or printer and rough cut 1 set.

TIP

Copy an extra set of patterns, and color the areas with crayons to correspond to the colors you'll use. This helps you keep track of your piecing.

A quick guide to surviving paper piecing:

1. The block pieces are numbered in the order in which they should be sewn.

2. For each numbered section, cut or use scraps that are at least ½˝ larger than the area shown.

3. Only sew along the lines shown. Don't sew into the seam allowances.

4. Spray starch is a wonderful friend when your block is finished and the paper is ready to be removed. Because there can be bias stretch from the fabric scraps, a spritz of starch followed by a hot iron will help stabilize the fabrics.

Instructions

1. Place the scrap for section 1 on the back of the paper with the fabric's wrong side facing the paper.

2. Hold the paper up to a light or window to check that the fabric covers all of section 1 with at least a ¼˝ overlap along all sides.

3. Place the scrap for section 2 with its right side facing the right side of scrap 1. Make the raw edge overlap the seamline by at least ¼˝.

4. Pin the 2 fabrics in place on the paper.

5. Flip the paper so the printed side is facing up, and place it under the sewing machine needle.

6. Stitch the line between sections 1 and 2 on the printed side with the fabric underneath. Clip the threads and remove the piece from the machine.

7. Flip over and fold the paper block template away from the stitched seam. Trim the seam allowances to ¼˝. Fold the paper back in place.

8. Flip scrap 2 over the seam so both pieces 1 and 2 face the correct direction with the fabrics right side up. Finger-press the seam between the 2 fabrics.

9. Hold the block to the light to check that scrap 2 covers its area.

10. Place the scrap for section 3 with its right side facing the right side of the previous piece and its raw edge again overlapping the seamline by at least ¼˝.

11. Pin scrap 3 in place on the paper.

12. Repeat Steps 5–9 to sew scrap 3 in place.

13. Continue repeating the process of placing, pinning, checking, sewing, and trimming for each numbered piece in order until they are all placed.

14. Trim the entire piece along the outer seam allowance line. Press the block well, and carefully remove the paper.

15. Sew each block's A and B sections together. Press the seam allowances open.

16. Sew the 2½″ × 6½″ rectangle to the top of the top block. Sew the 3½″ × 6½″ outer fabric rectangles to the sides.

17. Sew the left and right blocks together. Sew them to the top block section. Square up the finished block to 12½″ × 12½″.

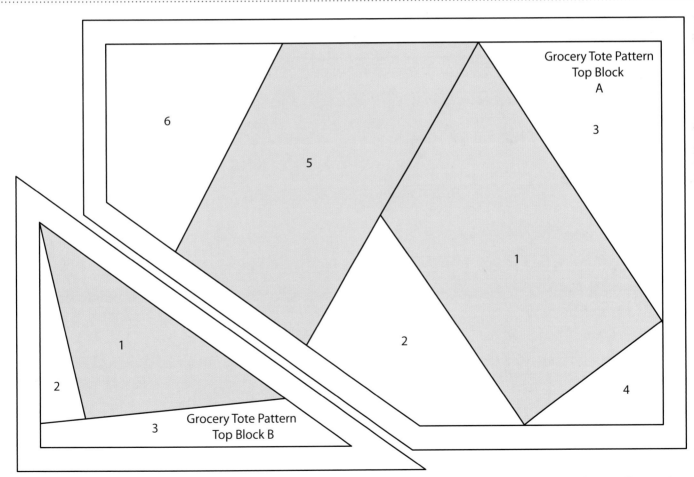

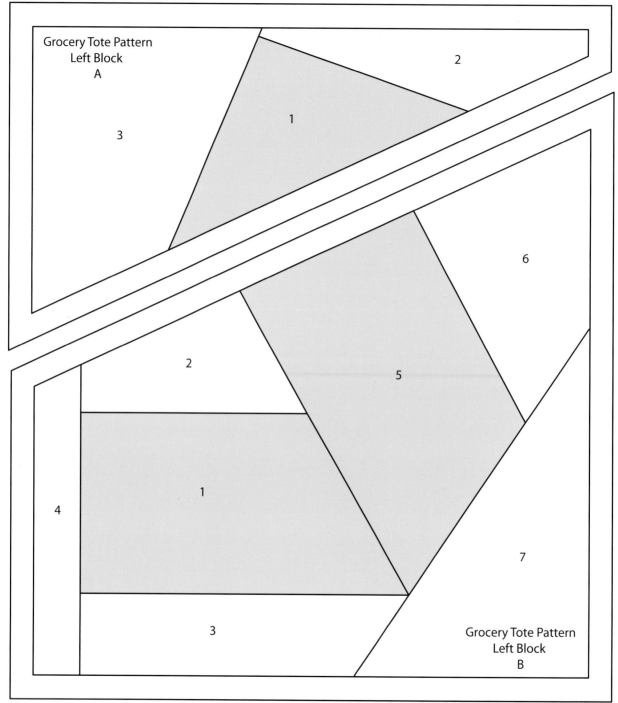

Grocery Tote Pattern
Left Block
A

3

1

2

6

2

5

1

4

3

7

Grocery Tote Pattern
Left Block
B

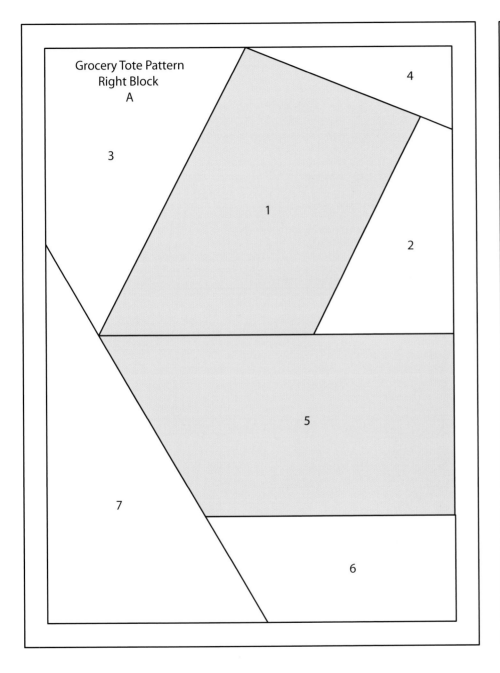

Grocery Tote Pattern
Right Block
A

3

4

1

2

5

7

6

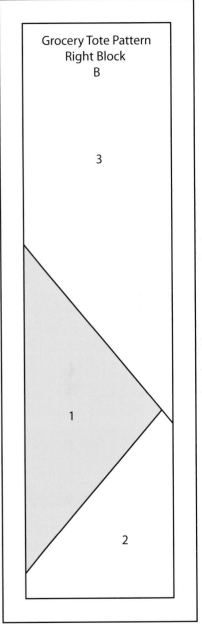

Grocery Tote Pattern
Right Block
B

3

1

2

Out-and-About BAG

At *GenQ*, we love bags! We keep making more, even though our closets are positively dripping with bags. When Sam offered us another bag, you gotta know we jumped at the chance. Sam uses only a few fabrics to keep this one simple, but we know that piecing the individual bag parts will give a scrappy look to this little pretty. And the flap is perfect for embellishment or embroidery.

Made by Sam Hunter

Finished size: 7˝ wide × 9˝ high × 2˝ deep

Artist: Sam Hunter
Website: huntersdesignstudio.com

Swap IDEAS

- According to our *GenQ* surveys on what we like to make, bags and purses come in second behind quilts! How about hosting a Just Bag It Swap, where each person makes a bag—any style, any size? It can be more personalized by having participants share features they like in their perfect bag (pockets, sized for e-readers, long instead of wide), or you can incorporate a detail from the bag's design to individualize.

- Have everyone use the exact same pattern as a starting point. Let creativity ensue.

Sam is a fiber artist and quilt designer who considers her sewing machine to be the ultimate power tool. She started sewing with her grandma when she was seven and hasn't really stopped since. She began quilting in 1989 and teaching shortly thereafter. She earned her MFA in Fibers in 2010 and is thrilled to have written her last-ever term paper. She launched her pattern design company, Hunter's Design Studio, in 2011 and will release a book with Stash Books in 2014.

MATERIALS AND SUPPLIES

Outer fabric: ½ yard

Lining fabric: ⅜ yard

Accent fabric: ⅓ yard

Pockets: ⅓ yard

Fusible batting: ¾ yard

2 D-rings 1½˝

2 swivel hooks 1˝

Magnetic closure

Template plastic or tracing paper

CUTTING

WOF = width of fabric

TIP

Label all the pieces with sticky notes or blue painter's tape as you cut them, indicating the top of each piece with an arrow.

Outer fabric

- Cut 2 rectangles 9½˝ × 10½˝ for the bag.
- Cut 1 strip 4˝ × WOF for the strap.
- Cut 1 strip 5˝ × 6˝ for the strap connectors.

Lining fabric

- Cut 2 rectangles 9¼˝ × 10¼˝ for the bag lining.
- Cut 1 rectangle 6½˝ × 8½˝ for the flap lining.

Accent fabric

- Cut 1 rectangle 6½˝ × 8½˝ for the flap.

Pocket fabric

- Cut 2 rectangles 9¼˝ × 10˝.

Fusible batting

- Cut 2 rectangles 9½˝ × 10½˝ for the bag.
- Cut 2 rectangles 9¼˝ × 10¼˝ for the bag lining.
- Cut 2 rectangles 6½˝ × 8½˝ for the flap.
- Cut 1 strip 2˝ × WOF for the strap.
- Cut 2 rectangles 4½˝ × 9½˝ for the pockets.

INSTRUCTIONS

All seam allowances are ¼˝. Press all seams open, unless noted. The flap pattern is on page 82. Trace and cut the pattern piece from tracing paper or template plastic.

······································

TIP

Using a walking foot on your sewing machine during the bag's construction will make life much easier. It helps keep the layers from slipping, ensuring more accurate sewing. If you don't have a walking foot, don't worry. Just use your regular sewing foot, and pin everything generously to maintain accuracy.

······································

Following the manufacturer's directions, iron fusible batting to the wrong sides of the fabric pieces for the outer bag, lining, flap, and flap lining.

Assemble the Strap

1. Cut the strap to the desired length. Between 38˝ and 40˝ is a good measurement for wearing on a shoulder. Between 42˝ and 44˝ is good for wearing cross-body.

2. Trim the fusible batting 6˝ shorter than the strap's length. Lay the fusible batting, sticky side down, along the strap fabric's center on the wrong side. Leave 3˝ of space at each end. (This is where the swivel hooks will be attached.)

3. Fold the long edges of the strap to the middle, covering the fusible fleece. Press.

4. Fold the strap lengthwise in half, right sides together, so the raw edges are folded inside. Press both sides to fuse them. Topstitch the strap along both long edges.

5. Thread an end of the strap through the swivel hook's ring. Fold under the raw edge of the end, and sew the end to the strap, just at the end of the fusible batting. Stitch across it 2–3 times. Repeat on the strap's other end.

6. Fold the long edges of the strap connector pieces to the middle of the wrong side and press. Fold the folded edges to the middle and press. Topstitch the long edges, and cut the piece in half to make 2 pieces 3˝ long.

7. Fold them in half lengthwise, and thread through the D-ring. Sew across the connector strap ends 2–3 times for added strength. Repeat with the second connector and D-ring.

Assemble the Pockets

1. Fold the pocket fabric lengthwise in half, wrong sides together, and press.

2. Unfold the pocket and nestle the fusible batting up to the fold. (Note: The batting is shorter than the fabric, so the gap you see at the bottom is correct.)

3. Refold the pocket fabric, and iron it to fuse the batting. Topstitch along the fold line to secure the batting and finish the edge. Repeat for the second pocket.

Pocket placement

1″

4. Cut a 1″ square from each bottom corner of both bag lining pieces. Mark a line ¾″ up from the top of the square cutouts on the right side of both pieces.

5. With the topstitched edge of the pocket facing down, place the raw edges on the chalked line.

6. Pin in place, centering the pocket on the lining piece. Sew a generous ¼″ from the raw edges, being sure not to catch the bottom edge of the batting inside the pocket. Repeat for the second pocket and lining piece.

7. Flip the pockets up so that the topstitched edge faces the top of the lining. Press. Draw chalk lines for the pocket sections onto the pockets. Mark the first line ¼″ in from the bottom cutouts. (This helps the bag maintain its square shape.) Mark the remaining pocket sections based on your preferences.

8. From the bottom to the top edges, sew the section lines for each pocket, being sure to backstitch.

Assemble the Parts

LINING

1. Sew the lining pieces, right sides together, on the sides. Then sew along the bottom, leaving a 3″ opening for turning. Press.

2. With the lining still inside out, box the corners by matching up the side and bottom seams and the raw edges of a cut corner. Sew and press. Repeat for the second corner. Turn the lining right side out.

OUTER BAG

1. Install the thicker half of the magnetic closure 3¼″ from the center top of an outer bag piece.

2. Cut a 1″ square from each bottom corner of both outer fabric pieces. Sew the bag pieces, right sides together, on the sides. Sew the bottom seam. Press.

3. Repeat Lining, Step 2, to box the outer bag corners.

FLAP

1. Place the inner and outer flap pieces right sides together, paying attention to the fabric's orientation. Pin them together. Use the pattern to mark the curved edge. Trim on the line. Stitch the curved edge.

2. Turn the piece right side out. Press well. Topstitch the curved edge.

3. Install the thinner half of the magnetic closure ¾″ from the center of the curved edge of the flap lining piece. (See the flap pattern for placement.)

Assemble the Bag

1. Identify the fronts and backs of the inner bag, outer bag, and flap. The outer bag front has the thick magnetic closure. The inner flap has the thin magnetic closure. Attach a sticky note on them if necessary. Check the pockets in the inner bag, and decide which will go to the back. Mark accordingly.

2. Turn the outer bag *right side in*. Turn the lining *right side out*.

3. With pins, mark the center of the flap's raw edge and the center of the bag's back raw edge. Then nest the flap into the outer bag, matching the flap's outer side to the outer bag's back. Line up the pins to center the flap; then baste the flap along the raw edges inside the ¼″ seam allowance.

4. Place a connector into the bag at the side seam, with the raw edge up and the D-ring down. Pin the connector's raw edge to the outer bag, centering it over the side seam and aligning the raw edges. Repeat with the second connector. Then baste the connectors along the raw edges inside the ¼″ seam allowance.

5. With the right side facing out, nest the lining into the outer bag, making sure the back pockets face the flap and the back of the bag. Align the side seams and raw edges, and pin generously. Stitch around the top of the bag.

TIP

Slow down your sewing speed as you sew across the thickest parts of the bag. Otherwise, you risk breaking needles.

6. Put your hand through the hole in the bottom of the bag, and pull the entire bag and strap through it. Press the seam between the inner and outer bag well, and then push the inner bag down into the outer bag. Press the seam again. Topstitch around the top of the bag. Stitch the opening at the bottom of the inner bag closed.

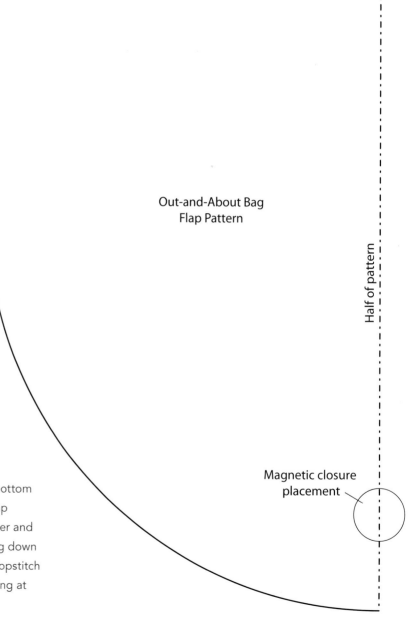

Out-and-About Bag
Flap Pattern

Half of pattern

Magnetic closure
placement

Doll's BED

Doll quilts are a great way to use up scraps, play with new techniques (such as fusible appliqué and free-motion quilting), and create something fast. Tracy happens to be a die-cut addict, and her circles and flower shapes were made using her cutting machine. We've provided the patterns for Tracy's shapes. The doll's pillow is an adorable bonus that we'd want to get with our quilts!

Made by Tracy Mooney

Finished sizes:

Quilt: 12˝ × 16˝

Pillow: 5˝ × 7˝

Pillowcase: 6˝ × 8˝

Swap IDEAS

- In person: Host a Make-It-Now Swap, where participants come together to create their doll quilts and share their fabric pieces. At the end of the day, the quilts are randomly drawn for keeps.

- Make toys the theme of your swap, and instead of giving them to each other, donate them to a children's hospital. Choose—vote or draw—a hospital in one or two of the towns of the participants, and send the projects to that participant to deliver.

- Provide precut shapes, and have participants work them into a design.

Tracy is associate editor of *Generation Q Magazine* and a freelance writer. At age four, a "keep the little one busy" project made her think that she was making a quilt, creating a lifelong obsession to follow through. She has been quilting for 22 years—although her husband would say there is way more obsessing than quilting going on some days. She has also been a professional actress and McAfee's chief cybersecurity mom.

MATERIALS AND SUPPLIES

White fabric: ½ yard for the quilt and pillowcase

Dark pink and green: scraps for the quilt

Print fabric: ½ yard for the quilt backing and pillowcase hem

Coordinating print: ¼ yard for the binding

Ticking stripe: fat quarter for the pillow

Dark pink: fat eighth for the pillowcase trim

Fusible web such as C&T's Make It Simpler Fusible Interfacing

Batting: 14″ × 18″

Polyfill for stuffing

CUTTING

WOF = width of fabric

White

- Cut 1 rectangle 12½″ × 16½″ for the quilt.
- Cut 1 rectangle 6½″ × 13″ for the pillowcase.

Print

- Cut 1 rectangle 14″ × 18″ for the quilt backing.
- Cut 1 rectangle 4½″ × 13″ for the pillowcase hem.

Coordinating print

- Cut 2 strips 2¼″ × WOF for the binding.

Ticking stripe

- Cut 1 rectangle 8″ × 11″ for the pillow.

Dark pink

- Cut 1 rectangle 1½″ × 13″ for the pillowcase trim.

INSTRUCTIONS

All seam allowances are ¼″. The patterns are on page 87. Trace the pattern pieces onto the fusible web's paper back, and rough cut them out. A flower pattern is included as an optional design.

Circle Quilt

1. Apply the fusible web shapes to the wrong side of the pink and green fabrics. Trace 1 large green circle, 2 medium green circles, 1 small green circle, 1 large pink circle, 1 medium-large pink circle, 1 medium pink circle, and 2 small pink circles. Follow the manufacturer's directions and fuse the web in place. Then cut the pieces out.

2. Arrange the circles randomly on the quilt as desired, and fuse them in place. If you're layering the circles, fuse the bottom circle first; then fuse the top circle to it.

FINISHING THE QUILT

1. Layer, baste, and quilt.

> ### TIP
> This is a great small project to practice free-motion quilting or play with some fancy threads!

2. Sew the binding strips end to end with diagonal seams. Trim the seam allowances to ¼˝ and press open. Press in half lengthwise with the wrong sides together.

3. Attach the binding to the quilt, mitering the corners. Overlap or seam the ends. Bring the folded edge to the back, and stitch it in place. (See C&T instructions for binding at ctpub.com > Resources > Consumer Resources: Quiltmaking Basics > How to Finish Your Quilt.)

Pillow

1. Fold the ticking stripe fabric in half to make a 5½˝ × 8˝ piece. Sew around the perimeter, leaving a 3˝ opening on a long side for stuffing.

2. Clip the corners and turn the pillow right side out. Stuff.

3. Close the opening by hand or machine.

Pillowcase

1. Fold the dark pink rectangle in half along the length, wrong sides together, and press.

2. Layer the white fabric, dark pink piece, and hem piece right sides together, lining up the raw edges along a 13″ side. Pin and sew. Press the seams toward the hem fabric.

3. Turn the pillowcase over, and fold the hem edge under ¼″. Press. Then fold it over again so the folded edge covers the seams.

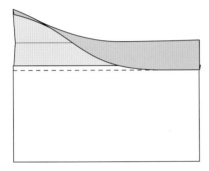

4. Turn the pillowcase over so the right sides face up, and pin along the seamline to secure the hem. Topstitch along the dark pink trim.

5. Fold the pillowcase right sides together, matching the hem. Sew along the bottom and long side. Zigzag stitch along the raw edges. Turn the pillowcase right side out and press.

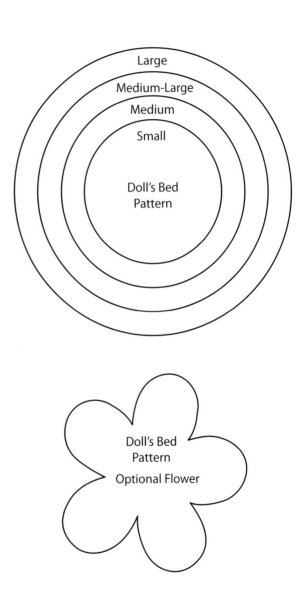

Interchangeable MONSTER

Irresistible! That's what we thought when we first saw this charming, adorable monster. What we like most is that this guy's body parts can be changed up and redone in cottons, linens, and other fabrics. Embellishments can be added to make the monster unique to you. It's just fun, and there's no reason we grown-ups can't enjoy a monster or two.

Made by Linda Hansen
Finished size: 5˝ × 9˝

Artist: Linda Hansen
Website: missmabelstudio.com

Swap IDEAS

- Approach this swap as a creativity challenge. Offer the basic monster pattern here, and encourage participants to change it to their liking.

- Make it an Embellishment Swap. Add buttons, glitter, snaps, rhinestones … more is more.

- Name your monster. In person, put the monsters' names on scraps of paper, and draw to see which one you take home.

- Or provide monster names before the crafting begins, and let the name be the inspiration for the monster created.

- An online facilitator can distribute names to participants via her favorite, most fair method. When all the monster pictures, with their names, are posted online (preferably before the drawing), participants will see which monster is coming to their house—that way they won't be scared!

Linda lives in a small town with her illustrious husband, Scott Hansen, of Blue Nickel fame. She also shares her space with three teens, three cats, one duck, and five chickens. A self-taught artist, Linda has made and played with dolls as long as she can remember. Her work has appeared in lots of books and magazines, but she considers the time spent with loved ones the best investment. When she is not herding children, cats, chickens, or husband (all of whom are impossible to give direction to) or playing with dolls, she blogs and sells her stuff at her Etsy shop, etsy.com/shop/MissMabel.

INSTRUCTIONS

The patterns are on page 91. Trace the patterns onto the freezer paper's paper side.

1. Rough cut the patterns from the freezer paper.

2. With your iron on the cotton setting, iron the pattern, plastic side down, to the felt.

3. Cut out the pattern piece on the line, and remove the freezer paper. You can reuse these pattern pieces several times.

4. Repeat Steps 1–3 for all the pieces. Cut 2 body pieces and 4 each of the other pieces.

5. Mark the button placement for the arms and legs. On the body, place a small square of wool on the wrong side of the body piece, and then place the button on the right side of the body piece. Sew the button on through both layers. The wool square reinforces the buttons.

6. Embroider and appliqué the face details. (Linda used a tiny button for the eye.)

7. Place the body front and body back wrong sides together, and then buttonhole stitch around the outside edges using perle cotton. Leave about a 1″ opening.

8. Lightly fill the body with stuffing. Sew the opening closed with a buttonhole stitch.

9. Use Fray Block on the edges.

10. Pair up the front and back pieces for each body part. Buttonhole stitch each pair, leaving a ½″ opening for stuffing.

11. Mark the buttonhole placement on the body parts, and carefully make a small slit that will hold the button through both layers of felt. Whipstitch around this slit. Lightly stuff the body parts using a hemostat. Close the seam with buttonhole stitching, and use Fray Block around the outer edges.

MATERIALS AND SUPPLIES

Wool felt: 10″ square

Wool felt scraps

Buttons

Perle cotton thread

Fray Block

Hemostat

Freezer paper

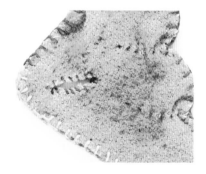

TIPS

• Do not stuff the wings. Stuffing will make them too stiff.

• Sew "feather" lines on the wings for texture.

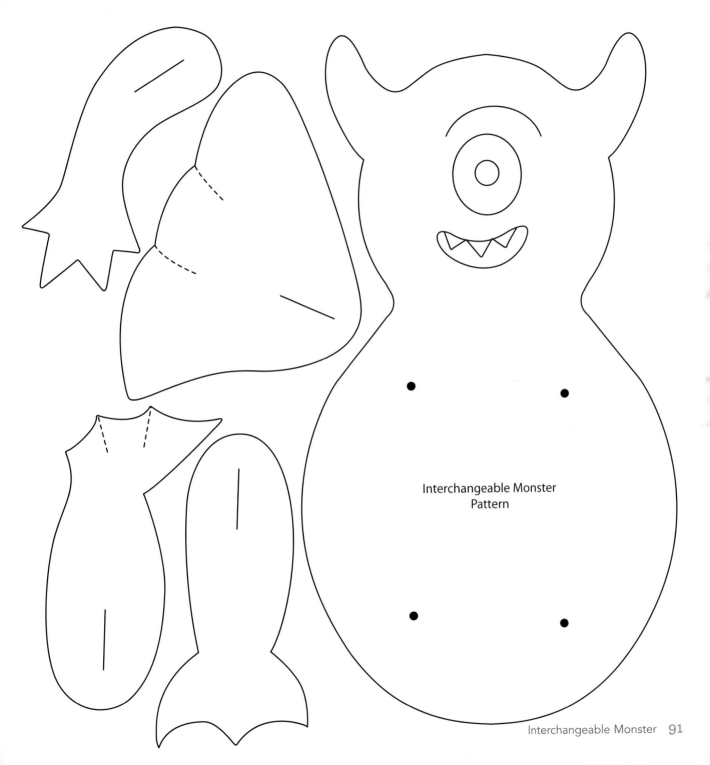

Interchangeable Monster
Pattern

Summer Reads BEACH BAG

Raise your hand if you think you can never have enough totes. Yep. That's what we thought. So here is a heavy-duty canvas creation designed to hoist books and supplies for your summer getaways. This lovely can be altered for any other purpose—and any season—so we're just getting you started here.

Made by Melissa Peda

Finished size: 15˝ wide × 12½˝ high × 5˝ deep

Artist: Melissa Peda
Website: 100billionstars.com

Swap IDEAS

- Totes are a great project to personalize for your swapee. With an unending supply of kitschy novelty fabrics around, form a swap where the swapper has to tailor a tote for the swapee's interests. Got an *I Love Lucy* lover? Grab the fabric and stitch away. How about an owl lover? Owl fabrics seem to be in a never-ending supply right now.

- Give this swap an added twist by having participants list three things about themselves that few people know—or place three small items that say something about them in the bag. Then, at the reveal, see who can match the tote to the recipient.

- Make seasons—spring, summer, fall, winter—part of your theme.

Melissa is a blogger, seamstress, crafter, quilter, designer, autodidact, book lover, coffee fiend, and more, who finds meaning and purpose in the "creative life." Color and creativity are two things she cannot live without. She is on a mission to inspire others to fill their own lives with heaps of both and frequently does this in her regular column in *GenQ*.

INSTRUCTIONS

Use a ½″ seam allowance unless otherwise stated.

1. Measure and mark 9″ from both 20″ edges of the outer bag fabric piece. Place the bottom fabric piece between the lines with both fabrics right sides up. Stitch in place ¼″ from the edges of the bottom piece.

2. Fold the outside pocket in half wrong sides together to create a 5″ × 6″ piece with the folded edge at the top. Press. Apply the optional appliqué to the pocket front, centering it carefully. With the pocket wrong sides together, topstitch along the folded edge.

3. Center the pocket on the outer bag, lining up the raw edges of the pocket on the raw edge of the bag bottom. Baste the pocket's sides in place ¼″ from the edges.

4. Place the webbing straps on the bag, beginning and ending at the raw edge of the bag bottom on each side and covering the raw edges of the pocket. Be careful not to twist the straps. The outside edges of the straps will be about 6¼″ from each side. Stitch the straps to the bag, stopping ⅝″ from the bag's top edge.

MATERIALS AND SUPPLIES

Dark blue print: ⅞ yard heavyweight canvas or home decorator print, 54″ to 60″ wide, for the outer bag

White print: ⅞ yard heavyweight canvas or home decorator print, 54″ to 60″ wide, for the outer bottom and lining

1½″ webbing: 3¼ yards

Contrasting fabric: 4″ × 4″ square (*optional*)

Fusible web: 4″ × 4″ square (*optional*)

CUTTING

Dark blue print

- Cut 1 rectangle 20″ × 30″ for the outer bag.

- Cut 1 rectangle 6″ × 10″ for the outside pocket.

- Cut 2 rectangles 10″ × 14″ for the inside pockets.

White print

- Cut 1 rectangle 12″ × 20″ for the outside bottom.

- Cut 1 rectangle 20″ × 30″ for the lining.

Webbing

- Cut 1 piece 42″ for the bag.

- Cut 2 pieces 36″ for the straps.

5. With right sides together, stitch the bag together at the sides. Press the seams open.

6. Create box corners on the bag's bottom by folding the bag at a corner, matching up the side seams and bottom fold to create a triangle. Use a ruler to find where the point measures 4″ across. Mark a line and sew on the line. Trim the excess fabric. Repeat with the other corner.

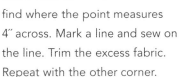

7. Turn the bag right side out. Pin the remaining piece of webbing around the bag, covering the raw edges of the bag bottom by at least ¼″. Stitch in place along both the top and bottom edges of the webbing, overlapping the ends and topstitching.

LINING

1. Measure and mark 11½″ from both 20″ edges of the lining piece for placement of the interior pockets. Using a nonpermanent fabric marker, draw a line across the lining piece from side to side at the marks.

2. Fold the short sides and top of an interior pocket over ¼″. Press. Topstitch around these 3 edges. Repeat for the second interior pocket, folding down the top edge more if desired.

3. Place the pocket wrong side up on the right side of the lining, with the raw edge at the marked line. Stitch in place using a ¼″ seam allowance. Fold the pocket so the right side is up. Press. Topstitch the side and bottom edges. Create the pocket divisions as desired, using a nonpermanent marker to mark the divisions. Stitch along the marked straight lines from top to bottom of the pocket piece. Repeat for the other side of the lining.

4. With right sides together, stitch the lining together at the sides, leaving a 4″ opening for turning. Press the seams open. Box the corners following the directions for the outer bag.

ASSEMBLY

1. With the bag right side out and the lining wrong side out, place the bag inside the lining. Pin and sew around the top edges, being careful to keep the straps away from the seams.

2. Turn the bag inside out through the opening in the lining. Press the bag's top edge. Topstitch the edge. Topstitch ¼″ from the edgestitching.

3. Stitch to close the opening.

Twofold Twist WALL QUILT

Made by Victoria Findlay Wolfe
Finished size: 21˝ × 29˝

Because we are primarily quilters, we have to swap quilts. But where do we start when there are infinite possibilities? Let's look at a swap's criteria:

• Needs to be a fast project

• Needs to be simple to create for the newbies

• Needs some kind of unifying theme

We say let's start with a wall quilt and see where that leads! Victoria's wonderful quilt packs quite the punch with its bold graphics and strong colors. But it's the long-stitch quilting that really makes us sigh. It adds texture and something soft to the design.

Swap IDEA

Working with a technique theme, coordinate a swap that features a specific pattern or stitch—like Victoria's long stitching—on a wall quilt. Set guidelines for the quilt's size (many times it's easier to give an overall minimum and maximum inch count for the total of all of the quilt's sides), and offer links, handouts, or a short workshop on doing long stitch. Because this is a quilt, consider a longer time frame for finishing the event.

Victoria is a New York City–based quilter and fabric designer. She is the author of *15 Minutes of Play* (C&T Publishing), founder of NYC Metro MOD quilters, and board member of the Quilt Alliance and International Quilt Association, and runs several community drives with Bumble Beans Basics. Born and raised on a farm in Minnesota, she credits her quilt obsession to her grandmother's double-knit crazy quilts that kept her warm while she was growing up. Her biggest supporters are her husband and daughter.

CUTTING

WOF = width of fabric

MATERIALS AND SUPPLIES

Pink solid: 8″ × 8″ scrap

Blue solid: 8″ × 8″ scrap plus ¼ yard for the binding

Lime solid: ½ yard

Red solid: ⅜ yard

Backing: ¾ yard

Batting: 25″ × 33″

12-weight perle cotton in pink, lime, blue, and red

Pink

- Cut 2 rectangles 3¼″ × 7″.

Blue

- Cut 2 rectangles 3¼″ × 7″.
- Cut 3 strips 2½″ × WOF for the binding.

Lime

Cut 6 strips 2″ × WOF.

Cut strips into:

- 8 rectangles 2″ × 3¼″ for the blocks.
- 8 rectangles 2″ × 10″ for the blocks.

- 2 rectangles 2″ × 18″ for the border.
- 2 strips 2″ × 29½″ for the border.

Red

Cut 5 strips 2″ × WOF.

Cut strips into:

- 8 rectangles 2″ × 6¼″ for the blocks.
- 8 rectangles 2″ × 13″ for the blocks.
- 2 rectangles 2″ × 9¼″ for the blocks.

INSTRUCTIONS

All seam allowances are ¼″.

This quilt is made from 2 pink blocks and 2 blue blocks. A block of each color is left intact. The second block of each color is cut down into other sizes and added to the other blocks. Press all the seams away from the centers of the blocks.

1. Sew the 2″ × 3¼″ lime rectangles to the ends of the pink and blue 3¼″ × 7″ rectangles.

2. Sew the 2″ × 10″ lime rectangles to the long edges of the pink and blue rectangles.

3. Sew the 2″ × 6¼″ red rectangles to the ends of the blocks.

4. Sew the 2″ × 13″ red rectangles to the long edges of the blocks.

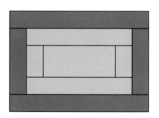

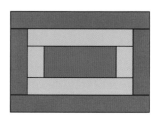

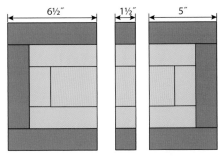

5. Cut 1 of each color of block in half crosswise to make 2 pieces 6½″ × 9¼″.

6. From the cut edge of a half-block of each color, cut a section 1½″ wide.

7. Sew the 2″ × 9¼″ red rectangles to a long edge of the 1½″ sections.

8. Arrange and sew the blocks in 2 vertical rows. Join the rows.

9. Sew the 2″ × 18″ lime border pieces to the top and bottom. Press the seams toward the border. Sew the 2″ × 29½″ lime border pieces to the sides. Press the seams toward the border.

10. Layer the backing, batting, and top. Baste the layers.

11. Use long stitches to quilt throughout the entire quilt. Victoria echo quilted around the blocks with casual long stitches. The stitches are about ¼″ to ½″ long and have about ½″ between them. The soft effect comes from the not-perfectly-straight lines, so don't worry about getting them perfect.

12. Sew the binding strips end to end with diagonal seams. Trim the seam allowances to ¼″ and press open. Press in half lengthwise with the wrong sides together.

13. Attach the binding to the quilt, mitering the corners. Overlap or seam the ends. Bring the folded edge to the back and stitch in place. (See C&T instructions for binding at ctpub.com > Resources > Consumer Resources: Quiltmaking Basics > How to Finish Your Quilt.)

Assembly diagram

Modern Broken Dishes TABLE SET

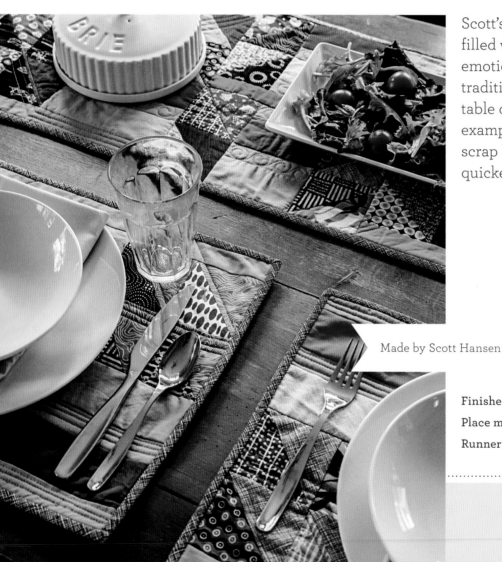

Scott's designs are always filled with riotous color and emotion, yet worked around traditional blocks. These table dressings are perfect examples. They are great scrap busters and work up quicker than they appear to.

Made by Scott Hansen

Finished sizes:
Place mat: 13½˝ × 18½˝
Runner: 13½˝ × 46½˝

Artist: Scott Hansen
Website: bluenickelstudios.com

Swap IDEAS

- In person: It's time for a Scrap Swap! Gather scraps from everyone, and make up bags of scraps for each participant. (You can do this for an online swap group; it's just going to take a little more dedication.) The scraps must be used in a project. Maybe you will allow sewists to add one or two additional fabrics to the mix. Maybe you won't!

- Online: Use your own scraps, but be considerate of the likes and dislikes of the person you're making the item for.

Scott has been in love with color as long as he can remember. He remembers the day he got that box of 64 Crayola crayons like it was yesterday. He learned to sew in junior high and made his first quilt at the age of 14. He left the needle for books for about 10 years, but wound his way back to quilting because it was faster than counted cross-stitch and left fewer splinters than woodworking. He has a beautiful wife, three amazing kids, three cats, three acres, and a plethora of poultry. Oh, and he still likes books. He wishes he were tidier in his workspace. (So does his wife.) He's also the community editor for *Generation Q Magazine*.

MATERIALS AND SUPPLIES

Makes 2 place mats and a table runner

Gold solid: ⅓ yard for the sashing

Solid scraps: ½ yard total for the blocks

Print scraps: ½ yard total for the blocks

Tonal scraps: ½ yard total for the blocks

Black print: ¾ yard for the binding

Backing: 2 yards

Batting: 2 pieces 15″ × 20″ each, 1 piece 15″ × 48″

CUTTING FOR ONE PLACE MAT

WOF = width of fabric

Solid gold

- Cut 3 rectangles 1½″ × 6½″.
- Cut 2 strips 1½″ × 18½″.

Solid scraps

- Cut 6 rectangles 2½″ × 6½″.

Three print scraps

- Cut 6 squares 3⅞″ (2 from each print); then cut each in half diagonally for 12 triangles.

Other print scraps

- Cut 6 squares 3⅞″; then cut each in half diagonally for 12 triangles.

Black print

- Cut 2 strips 2½″ × WOF for place mat binding.

CUTTING FOR RUNNER MIDDLE SECTION

Solid gold

- Cut 4 rectangles 1½″ × 4½″.

Solid scraps

- Cut 4 rectangles 2½″ × 4½″.
- Cut 1 strip 1½″ × 10½″.

Print scraps

- Cut 8 squares 3⅞″; then cut them in half diagonally, making a total of 16 triangles.

Black print

- Cut 4 strips 2½″ × WOF for table runner binding.

Place Mat
INSTRUCTIONS

All seam allowances are ¼˝.

1. Sew the solid scrap rectangles to either side of the gold rectangles. Press away from the gold rectangles. Make 3 units.

2. Sew 4 triangles of the same fabric to 4 triangles of different prints.

3. Sew 4 triangle units together to make a single unit. Make 3 of these units. (Fig. 1)

4. Arrange and sew the units into 3 vertical rows. Press. Join the rows. Press. (Fig. 2)

5. Add the gold 1½˝ × 18½˝ rectangles to the long edges. Press. (Fig. 3)

6. Layer the back (wrong side up), batting, and top (right side up). Baste. Quilt as desired. Trim to 13½˝ × 18½˝.

7. Sew the binding strips end to end with diagonal seams. Trim the seam allowances to ¼˝ and press open. Press in half lengthwise with the wrong sides together.

8. Attach the binding to the quilt, mitering the corners. Overlap or seam the ends. Bring the folded edge to the back, and stitch it in place. (See C&T instructions for binding at ctpub.com > Resources > Consumer Resources: Quiltmaking Basics > How to Finish Your Quilt.)

Fig. 1

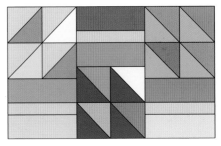

Fig. 2

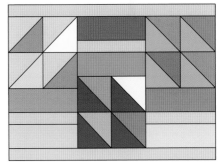

Fig. 3

Runner

The Modern Broken Dishes Runner is made from 2 place mat units with a middle section added. Instructions follow for the middle section.

INSTRUCTIONS

1. Sew 2 place mat units using the previous instructions.

2. Sew 2 solid scrap rectangles and 2 gold rectangles together to make a unit. Press away from the gold rectangles. Make 2 units.

3. Sew 16 triangles together to make 8 half-square triangles. Sew them together in pairs, with the diagonal of 2 pairs in 1 direction and the other 2 pairs in the opposite direction. Press the seams open. Make 4 pairs.

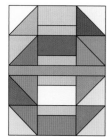

4. Arrange and sew the rectangle units to the triangle units. Press toward the rectangle units. Sew to each side of the 1½″ × 10½″ rectangle to make the middle section.

5. Sew the 2 place mat sections to each side of the middle section.

6. Layer the backing, the batting, and the top. Baste. Quilt as desired. Trim to 13½″ × 46½″.

7. Refer to Steps 7 and 8 in Place Mat (page 103) to bind the table runner.

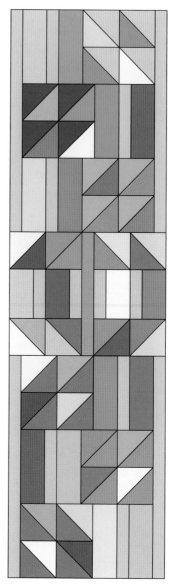

Assembly diagram

Heartbeat COUCH SCARF

Made by Anne Deister

Finished size: 24″ × 48″

Okay, this really is just a long, pretty quilt. But it was designed specifically to dress up a plain leather couch, where it can spread out horizontally or pretty up the center cushion. It also could be used on walls or a large table. Make a larger one for snuggling under! Low-volume quilts are a current trend in the Q-niverse. Low volume is really low contrast, and these prints—while not tone on tone—are close, with their white backgrounds and gray or black designs. The variety of prints is what makes this quilt delicious.

Artist: Anne Deister
Website: springleafstudios.com

Swap IDEA

We've all got areas in our home that are a little funky to dress up, so why not have a funky swap? Each participant offers a problem area of his or her home with measurements, a couple of color choices, and maybe even a picture, and the swapper works up a quilt around those parameters.

Anne birthed SpringLeaf Studios as a way to merge her graphic design background with her fabric addiction. Publishing quilt patterns seemed like a great way to put that ever-expanding stash to use. Little did she know her stash would simply grow. Her quilt designs are based on strong graphics and bold color, and often include large-scale prints. Anne's love of design is evident in her versatile patterns, which include optional "design explorations" meant to encourage quilters to explore their own creativity.

MATERIALS AND SUPPLIES

Varied white background prints: 28 or more strips of fabrics 2½″ × 21″

Accent prints: 28 or more 2½″ × 5″ rectangles

Narrow stripe: ⅜ yard for the binding

Backing: 1⅝ yards

Batting: 28″ × 52″

CUTTING

WOF = width of fabric

Narrow stripe
- Cut 4 strips 2½″ × WOF for the binding.

Backing
- Cut 1 rectangle 28″ × 52″.

INSTRUCTIONS

All seam allowances are ¼″.

Note: Anne uses a stitch-and-flip technique along with a quilt-as-you-go technique for easy construction.

TIP
You'll be sewing strips and quilting at the same time, so your stitches will show on the back. Choose a thread color to match the backing.

1. Using a design wall or large flat area (you can spread a large piece of flannel on a dining table and then hold it up), arrange the white strips in a pleasing arrangement so that prints and values are distributed evenly.

2. Add accent pieces on top of the strips, balancing the color distribution. Stagger the placement of the accent pieces by positioning them on either side of the center in a pleasing, random order.

3. Gently fold the accent pieces in half in order to mark where to cut the background strips. Cut the background strips, and sew the accent pieces between the 2 ends. Press the seams toward the accent fabrics.

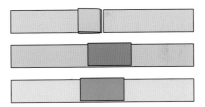

4. When all are sewn, reposition the strips in the correct order on the design wall.

TIP
Take a quick picture of the arrangement before sewing so you can remember what you did.

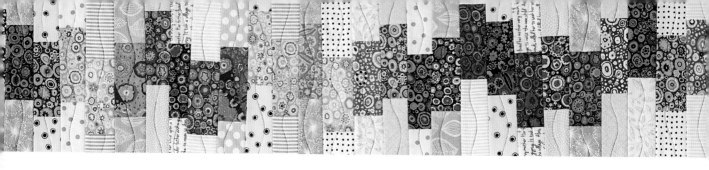

5. Baste the backing and batting together.

6. Position the first pieced strip, right side up, about 1″ from the top edge of the backing/batting sandwich, making sure the strip is parallel to the top edge. Sew along the top edge to secure it to the batting and backing.

7. Position the next strip, right side down, over the first strip and at a slight angle. Pin it in place. Sew along the edge of the second strip.

8. Trim away the excess fabric from each seam, and press the strip well so it lies flat before attaching the next strip. This is important, or you might end up with a bubble that can't be flattened.

9. Continue adding strips.

> ### NOTES
>
> ▶ As you add strips, make sure the strips line up along an edge as evenly as possible. Because you're sewing each strip at an angle, the entire piece can start to skew if you are not watching for it.
>
> ▶ Depending on the angles, you may need more or fewer than the given number of strips. Adjust accordingly, or simply make your runner longer or a bit shorter.

10. When there are only 3 strips left to sew, measure from the first strip and mark a line parallel to the top edge with tape. Continue adding the last strips, working toward making the last strip parallel to the tape.

11. Trim to straighten the side edges.

12. Sew the binding strips end to end with diagonal seams. Trim the seam allowances to ¼″ and press open. Press in half lengthwise with the wrong sides together.

13. Attach the binding to the quilt, mitering the corners. Overlap or seam the ends. Bring the folded edge to the back and stitch in place. (See C&T instructions for binding at ctpub.com > Resources > Consumer Resources: Quiltmaking Basics > How to Finish Your Quilt.)

Beach Glass PILLOW TOP

Even the most basic pillow fashioned out of an incredible fabric will update a tired room. Heather's pillow couldn't be simpler, but what makes this a standout is the quilting framing the colored strips.

Made by Heather Jones

Finished size: 18˝ × 18˝

Artist: Heather Jones
Website: oliveandollie.com

Swap IDEAS

- In person, let's play Pass the Jelly Roll, the swap where participants each bring 9 strips of fabric, 2½″ × 40″, and throw them into a bag. Each person then draws out 9 strips and is allowed to add one more fabric in any amount to the mix. That's what they get to work with, folks, and there's a lot of creativity that comes from a swap like this!

- Online: Send strips to participants. Get creative. Send 3 strips to 3 different people.

Heather is a designer and modern quilter who lives outside of Cincinnati, Ohio, with her husband and two young children. She founded the Cincinnati chapter of the Modern Quilt Guild, and three of her original quilts were chosen as winners of the Modern Quilt Guild's Project Modern Challenges, a year-long national quilting competition. Heather teaches quilting workshops throughout the country, and her work has been featured in many publications.

MATERIALS AND SUPPLIES

Different colored solids:
9 strips 2½″ × 10½″ each

Gray fabric: 1 yard for borders and backing

Batting: 20″ × 20″

Backing: 20″ × 20″

Premade pillow form:
18″ × 18″ square

CUTTING

Gray

- Cut 2 rectangles 4½″ × 18½″ for the borders.

INSTRUCTIONS

All seam allowances are ¼″.

1. Sew 9 solid strips together along the long sides. Press all the seams open.

2. Sew the gray strips to the top and bottom of the pieced center. Press the seams open.

3. Layer the pillow top backing, batting, and pillow top to make a quilt sandwich. Baste as desired.

4. Quilt as desired.

TIPS

- Heather quilted in the gray pieces with coordinating threads, but you can have fun with more detailed quilting and specialty threads.

- Put a different quilting pattern in each strip, and really practice your skills!

5. Trim the quilted top to 18½″ × 18½″.

PILLOW BACK

For instructions on how to do the backs of pillows, go to GenerationQMagazine.com/StitchNSwap.

stash BOOKS ®

fabric arts for a handmade lifestyle

If you're craving beautiful authenticity in a time of mass-production...Stash Books is for you. Stash Books is a line of how-to books celebrating fabric arts for a handmade lifestyle. Backed by C&T Publishing's solid reputation for quality, Stash Books will inspire you with contemporary designs, clear and simple instructions, and engaging photography.

www.stashbooks.com